DEVELOPMENTAL DESIGNS SELF-COACHING GUIDE

Reflection, Feedback, and Strategies for High Student Engagement

TODD BARTHOLOMAY   **ERIN KLUG**   **SCOTT TYINK**

ISBN: 978-0-938541-23-3

Library of Congress Control Number: 2014907928

Photography by Karl Herber and John Goebel

Illustrations, cover and book design by Heidi Neilson

Editors: Jo Devlin and Elizabeth Crawford

The Origins Program
3805 Grand Avenue South
Minneapolis, Minnesota 55409
800-543-8715

www.developmentaldesigns.org

18 17 16 15 14   5 4 3 2 1

ACKNOWLEDGMENTS

We are grateful to the educators who contributed their *Developmental Designs* practice wisdom to this book's content and who piloted its use. Without your insights and collaboration this self-coaching tool would not have taken its rich and practical shape.

Rob Jagers and Terrance Kwame-Ross, for expert guidance in designing and executing the book's pilot study.

Edna Attias, Josie Batista, Janet D'Ambrosio, Molly Rosen, Victoria Tolbert-Bravo, and Sara VanDeWalker, for taking the time and effort to pilot this tool in their classrooms, including video-recording and indispensable feedback on the process.

Jennifer Griffin-Wiesner, for facilitating the pilot, including conducting meaningful and respectful interviews with participants.

Christopher Hagedorn, Sharon Greaves, and Roxanne Hable, for contributing practice insights and language at critical points.

Elizabeth Crawford, for shepherding this tool through re-conceptualizations and myriad revisions while tenaciously insisting that it be teacher-friendly and practical.

Jo Devlin, for rigorously minding the details of language and the core ideas of our work.

Heidi Neilson, for her patience and inventive design and illustration bringing energy and order to our manuscripts.

The lively presence of teachers and students on the book's cover would not be possible without the collaboration of Robert Barry and his advisory group at Maplewood Middle School in Minnesota, and Victoria Tolbert and her students at Paul Cuffee School in Rhode Island.

We acknowledge teachers working doggedly in their classrooms to cultivate practices that engage every student reliably and productively. May this tool assist them in seeing what may be hidden, in self-guidance, and in collaboration with teammates toward that end.

—Todd Bartholomay, Erin Klug, and Scott Tyink

Table of Contents

CHAPTER ONE

Introduction

This *Guide* is designed to help teachers coach themselves—that is, gain useful feedback on their own, without outside professional coaching—to spur their growth as educators. The tool is founded on more than a decade of professional *Developmental Designs* coaching, presenting the practical supports most useful to teachers.

When *Developmental Designs* is implemented by a team, the *Self-coaching Guide* can anchor and foster feedback-rich conversations in professional learning communities, team meetings, and professional-development meetings.

How can I improve my Developmental Designs practice?

Feedback—descriptive information about the qualities of practice related to goals—is a powerful tool for learning.[1] This Guide empowers teachers to gather self-feedback to become more aware of their teaching practices, to define growth targets, to prioritize and focus their efforts to reach their targets, and to reflect on their process and progress.

Consider how researcher/educator Grant Wiggins defines feedback: "Feedback is not evaluation, the act of placing value. Feedback is value-neutral help on worthy tasks. It describes what the learner did and did not do in relation to her goals. It is actionable information, and it empowers the student to make intelligent adjustments when she applies it to her next attempt to perform."[2]

The *Guide* makes progress toward practice goals transparent, and then provides strategies—actionable information—for adjusting practice closer to the goal. As practice evolves over time, progress it again noted and new strategies apply.

Learning Loop

The Loop—action, reflection, planning, and further action—taught in the *Developmental Designs* I workshop helps students become aware of and make choices about their learning. Similarly, using the Loop to strategize, act, and reflect helps educators plan and review their teaching. In both cases, the Loop helps learners see, understand, prioritize, and grow, and can be integrated into daily practice for daily growth. This learning cycle creates continuous, endless growth—social, academic, and emotional for students, professional for educators—at practical, daily levels.

Just as *Developmental Designs* strives for intrinsic learning and motivation in students, this *Guide* empowers teachers to observe and analyze their own practice and to increase their efficacy. It is a tool for setting a course of action to grow in effectiveness. It is an affirmative, teacher-friendly tool for building on one's strengths and fostering practice capacity.

The *Guide's* feedback process addresses common implementation questions:

What does this practice look like when fully implemented?

What student responses will indicate that I'm on the right track?

What's in the way of my progress?

What are some strategies to tackle this challenge?

What should I focus on next?

How should I use this Guide? Where should I start?

Educators use the *Guide* differently depending on their needs; possibilities for your use of it will become clearer as you become familiar with it. It is meant to be personalized.

A way to create a strong start is to first review and resolve to engage the three teacher mindsets described in Chapter Two: Mindsets Create the Tone of Teaching. Foundational to effective teaching is:

- having faith in every student's ability to grow (the growth mindset);
- seizing opportunities and advocating for growth (the action mindset); and
- not taking things personally or allowing emotions to obscure the best action (the objective mindset).

Reviewing these productive mindsets is never a waste of time; they underlie everything we do and are essential for effective communication with students.

The following lists elements in the cycle of self-coaching. As an educator becomes experienced in self-coaching, s/he might use some or all of these elements in this or another order:

1) Reflecting on practice relative to goals

2) Recognizing strengths and areas for growth

3) Identifying obstacles to growth

4) Reviewing and selecting strategies for growth

5) Implementing strategies

6) Noting effects of implemented strategies

Prepare for best use of the reflection tool: Read through the reflection questions ahead of time on the day you plan to review your practice. The questions help raise awareness of best practice and will sharpen your observations: Do my students use eye contact during the greeting? Do students return from TAB refocused on learning? Do I balance redirecting and reinforcing language?

Use video recording to strengthen observation: We emphasize the importance of "noticing" as teachers because unless we aware of what is going on we cannot address it. When it comes to refining instruction, there is no substitute for seeing with our own eyes what happens in our classrooms. Reviewing a video recording of your practice and students' responses helps you see with greater clarity the effects of your behaviors as well as some of the small things—facial expressions, gestures, background activity, etc.—that may otherwise be unseen when relying solely on memory. Using video with the *Self-coaching Guide* will give you an unfiltered picture of your strengths and areas for growth and help reveal any misconceptions you might have.

Individual use of this *Guide*

Consider one or more elements of your *Developmental Designs* practice, identifying strengths and areas for growth. After identifying obstacles to success and strategies you will use, define a period of implementation, including cycles of reflection, strategy, and action.

Use the *Guide's* tools flexibly, depending on your needs. For example, the barriers sections are designed to help direct you to strategies most likely to support your growth, but you may prefer to search a strategies section, top to bottom, for an approach that will leverage your practice.

You might choose to schedule regular times to record yourself in the classroom, then review your classroom practice using the *Guide* to help you notice proficiencies and gaps in practice. You could set up a schedule of exchange visits and supportive feedback with a colleague.

Wherever and however you begin using the *Guide*, make frequent use of the Loop—reflection, strategy, and action—to keep your target clearly before you amid the distractions of school life.

Team use of this *Guide*

This *Guide* can anchor professional learning communities and other staff gatherings focused on professional growth. Since several teachers typically work with each student in a middle school, aligning routines and core practices throughout a team increases consistency and reduces stress for students and improves efficiency for everyone. Using this *Guide*, teacher teams can reflect on progress, create common practice goals, identify useful shared strategies, and pull, like a team of horses, in the same direction.

Example of a team use: Before the start of the school year, the seventh-grade team reviews data from the previous year and considers the apparent academic and social needs of the students they will soon begin to work with. They look for groups and/ or individuals who were especially successful, and identify teacher behaviors that may have supported their success and can be continued in the coming year.

They also consider groups or individuals who were unsuccessful, and think about and discuss teacher behaviors that may have contributed to their failure, and teacher practices that might engage these students for growth in the coming year. Using this *Guide*, they identify one or more *Developmental Designs* practices that would be relevant to the students' apparent needs. Each teacher reflects on the quality of her/ his practice using the relevant *Guide* Reflecting tool (e.g., Reflecting on Advisory, page 31). S/he identifies strengths and areas for growth, considers possible obstacles to growth, and finds in the *Guide* strategies that would apply. The entire team creates a clear, specific action plan to support each other's strategy implementation for a certain period of time through peer visits and/or sharing videos.

The team meets bi-weekly to share implementation successes, questions, or problems. They visit each other's rooms as planned to provide helpful feedback on one another's practice. At the end of the initial implementation time, the team uses the reflection tool to see what gains were made, to share successes and challenges, and to strategize for continued growth. This cyclical process continues through the year, including looking at student response to the practices. At the end of the school year, the team reflects on their growth and on persistent or new challenges, and they make a preliminary plan for the next year's beginning focus.

Interconnected nature of the practices

Because the practices of *Developmental Designs* are interrelated, any of them can be a starting point and will sooner or later connect with all the others, creating a consistent, positive pedagogy and learning environment. Advisory is especially supported by effective implementation across practices. The purposes of advisory include community-building and social-skills growth that can only be realized through relationship-based pedagogy—the same pedagogy that transforms content classes and engages students. For this reason, advisory is a great place to begin implementing the practices. A teacher who masters the practices in the advisory context can then bring the relationship-based strategies into his or her academic classes with confidence.

A teacher's vision of a true classroom community of learners can be realized by using this resource over time with confidence. As you begin your self-coaching experience, we wish you every success in your commitment to better teaching!

---

1 "In a recent update of Marzano, Pickering, and Pollock's 2001 meta-analysis, McREL researchers found an effect size for feedback of 0.76, which translates roughly into a 28 percent improvement in average achievement (Beesley & Apthorp, 2010; Dean, Pitler, Hubbell, & Stone, 2012). John Hattie (2009) found a similar effect size of 0.73 for feedback in his synthesis of 800 meta-analyses of education research studies; in fact, feedback ranked among the highest of hundreds of education practices he studied." Bryan Goodwin and Kirsten Miller, "Good Feedback Is Targeted, Specific, and Timely," Educational Leadership 70 (September 2012): 82.

2 Grant Wiggins, "Feedback: How Learning Occurs, May 22, 2010" Authentic Education, *Big Ideas*, https://www.authenticeducation.org/ae_bigideas/article.lasso?artId=61.

Mindsets Create the Tone of Teaching

"Teaching, like any truly human activity, emerges from one's inwardness, for better or for worse."[1]

A classroom lesson is composed of many crucial elements: the content of the lesson; the format of instruction; the learning that has come before the lesson and the learning that will follow it; remembering facts, honing skills, provoking thought; the subtleties of communication; behavior that requires corrective action; and more.

And a lesson is powerfully influenced by the thoughts and feelings of the teacher and the learners. Everything that transpires in a classroom is affected by the frames of mind of the people in the classroom. For example, students who live in poverty and/or violence bring their after-effects into school. Teachers who are excited about their subjects bring their eager energy, and teachers who are overwhelmed by demands at home or at school express that state of mind. Our mindset is the background behind everything we do and say in the classroom.

The extent to which we can help our students develop the social-emotional and academic skills that are crucial to their success depends on our using productive mindsets. Specifically, the mindsets most crucial to teaching effectiveness are:

Growth mindset

The space of possibility that we hold for all our students—our belief in their capacity for growth into responsible independence as we guide them—and the cultivation of this belief within the students themselves. Teacher: *I know that change and growth are possible for everyone, everywhere, all the time.* Student: *I know that through effort I can grow. I know that my teacher believes I can grow.*

Action mindset

The active support of each student through good times and bad, which means a commitment of heart and mind fueled by courage and a sense of urgency: *I am motivated by determination to generate ways for my students to grow.*

Objective mindset

The ability to interact with students without taking what they do and say personally: *I work to keep a cool head and a warm heart in the face of disappointment and conflict.*

No matter what teaching strategy we are employ, our state of mind—our thoughts and feelings, the mental explanations we make for what is going on at any moment—helps determine how things turn out. For example, it's useless to model for students how you want them to share their ideas or experiences in an advisory meeting unless you believe they can learn to share articulately, and you are determined to help them get it, no matter how crabby or silly they may act, even when they irritate you. The teacher's mindset makes all the difference in whether and how learning takes place.

GROWTH MINDSET

Teaching is most successful when the teacher believes in the capacity of all people to grow, and when the teacher cultivates in the students a belief in their own growth. In other words, we must teach a growth mindset, model it, and hold the space for students who do not yet believe in themselves.

I was working with the sixth grade students on a writing assignment. They were told to think of an incident in their lives and then tell about it in short-story form. Devon sat and tapped a pencil and wrote nothing. "I can't do this," he said. I asked a few questions about his family, and he told me about putting up a fence with his dad. As he spoke, I wrote down what he said, and after a couple of minutes, I pointed to the paper. "There are your first two paragraphs. What happened next?" This time, I just listened, and then said, "Write that down, and you're almost done with the story. All that's left is to tell the readers how the fence turned out."

—Writer in residence for middle level students

Fixed and Growth Mindsets Compared

Consider the dangers of "fixed-mindset" thinking for adolescents: A physically awkward boy in his early teens had had several negative experiences on the playground. He lacked stamina, had poor hand-eye coordination, and bumped into others. He decided he was a klutz (a fixed mindset), and began to avoid physical activity. He soon reached his full height and became more coordinated. He might have discovered a love of Ultimate Frisbee or soccer and gone on to decades of healthful physical activity and the social benefits of team sports, had he held onto a growth mindset, but because he had settled into a mindset that labeled his athletic skills deficient, he lost out.

Interestingly, a fixed mindset is just as dangerous when it seems positive: An eighth grader did well in math and decided she was a math whiz (a fixed mindset) until she confronted algebra. Struggling with math for the first time in her life, she quickly felt incompetent, and swung to a new summary judgment: math wasn't really for her, after all. Chances are she simply wasn't developmentally ready to handle the abstract thinking required to integrate the algebraic mode, but by labeling herself first a winner, then a loser, in math, she deprived herself of possibilities.

The impact of growth and fixed mindsets was the focus of a study of low-achieving seventh graders in New York City. All the students in the group began by attending sessions during which they learned study skills, how the brain works, and other achievement-related topics. The control group attended an informational session on memory and discussed academic issues of personal interest to them, while the other group learned that intelligence, like a muscle, grows stronger through exercise. The group that received the growth-mindset messages greatly improved in the areas of motivation and math grades; students in the control group showed no improvement despite the other interventions.[2]

The mindsets we are discussing are social-emotional skills, not passive characteristics. The research shows the importance of having conversations with *all* students about how intelligence grows—through exercise and effort. As social skills are taught and practiced, mistakes can be viewed as opportunities to fix things and try again. Through encouragement and reflection, students experience their own growth, and perhaps establish for life the mindset that growth is not only possible, but likely, when the target is clear and the effort consistent.

Characteristics of Growth-minded Students

"When students believe they can develop their intelligence, they focus on doing just that. Not worrying about how smart they will appear, they take on challenges and stick to them."[3]

Growth-minded students
* believe they are capable of growth, even in the face of difficulty and setbacks
* emphasize the effort they bring to their work, not their talent; they identify as hard workers
* do not expect that past success or failure will determine future ability
* resist final judgment or labeling of themselves as skilled in one area or unskilled in another
* use the successes of others to inspire their effort instead of comparing and despairing

Characteristics of Growth-minded Teachers

Being growth-oriented in teaching means having the humility to acknowledge your own gaps while you move toward your growth objectives: *I don't know everything. There's still a lot for me to learn, and I can and will grow.* Such a stance keeps our minds open to learning from colleagues, workshops, books, and from students themselves, and infuses optimism into frustrating, potentially defeating moments: *I know this student can grow. What does he need from me to make this happen, and what do I need to learn about him?*

Recognizing that we don't know everything allows us to see more accurately the strengths in students that can be parlayed into independence and power, and strengths that are growing in ourselves to guide them there. It's like having a third eye to see what isn't there yet in our students and in ourselves. An apt adjustment of the old adage would be: *I'll see it when I believe it!*

Self-assessment is a useful tool for growth-minded teachers. They think about what they're going to do, do it, and then think about how well it went, planning improvements for next time. They do it on notes scribbled to themselves, in talks with colleagues, and on the drive home. They assess how they and their students are growing because they are ameliorators, always looking for ways to make good better and better best.

Growth-minded teachers

- believe effort, not talent, is the path to mastery
- believe every student has the capacity to grow and ultimately succeed, even when students resist learning
- teach self-control and resilience as learnable capacities (some students need more guidance than others)
- believe *they* have the capacity to grow in skill so that all students' needs can be addressed
- consistently assess what and how they teach, teacher-student relationships, and student growth
- see challenges and criticism as contexts for growth, and welcome them
- adopt a curious frame of mind when faced with challenges: *I wonder if it would help this student if I...*

Results of a Growth Mindset

Goal setting

Teachers use a growth mindset to write learning targets in student-friendly language to maximize clarity. They teach students to keep the learning targets in front of them all the time and are quick to acknowledge and describe movement toward the target, as well as learning still to be accomplished. The student consistently knows where she stands and where she's going, and believes that time and effort will get her there.

Advisory

Teachers use growth mindsets to plan advisory meetings that include all students, while making sure none are allowed to dominate. The participatory playing field becomes more balanced: extroverts learn self-control, while introverts learn to be more assertive; students learn about key social-emotional skills, such as self-control, resilience, and persistence, and practice them daily.

Formative modeling

A growth-oriented teacher plans exactly how she will model her routines for maximum student understanding. Equipped with a clear understanding of several basic routines, students are able to consistently and effectively execute the routines.

Empowering language

Students are empowered by growth-oriented teachers to think about their own behavior and make their own judgments. Teachers regularly ask themselves: *What can I say to this student that will help him grow?* The split-second thinking process might go something like: *Robert is focused and on-task today. How should I speak to him so he notices his accomplishment and uses it to continue to learn? I'll speak to his strength: "You seem extra energetic today, and you're channeling your energy into your learning. You are on your way to accomplishing both of the tasks and hitting the learning target."*

Effective Pathways to Self-control

Students learn to initiate and complete their own problem solving after receiving a cue from the teacher. To prime self-management, teachers explain why and how they will use Pathways. They ascertain which students benefit from which cue(s) and adjust their use accordingly. Teachers ask themselves when students break the rules: *How should I redirect this student so she can grow?* This split-second thinking process might go something like: *Gia just passed a note to Shay. I think I'll use Fix it on the Spot so she learns when it's OK to communicate with friends and when it's more important to keep her attention on the task at hand.* We believe that with guidance and perseverance, students grow toward responsible independence.

Warning Signs

Things can happen that halt growth and even negate its possibility. Repeated failure to perform, recurring loss of emotional or social controls, words spoken in anger, frustration, or mere haste—all endanger the growth mindset of teachers and students. If teachers find themselves frustrated to the point of giving up on a student; if students move toward hopelessness about success in school or in life; if the mood is one of constantly trying to catch up, not making progress, the mindsets of both teacher and students may start moving toward the idea that the way things are now is permanent and pervasive, and they personally feel resigned to failure. When negativity piles up, the growth mindset is under siege.

The response needed to get things moving again toward the targets is to note successes in the past, tally strengths, identify starting places, point again toward the desired outcome(s), and gather evidence that they (teacher and student) have succeeded in the past and can expect to do so again. Acknowledge the targets already achieved, and plot out a pathway toward those remaining. Use the Strategies sections in this book to build the bridges needed for growth, and watch for warning signs that someone has lost their way.

Strategies for Nurturing a Growth Mindset in Students

Language that encourages a growth mindset
Recognition of small evidence of growth after being stuck: *John, you made two comments during sharing in our CPR this week. Did you notice? I really enjoyed hearing your thoughts.*

Relevance of strengths in other areas compared to stuck places: *Sharon, the determination you show in basketball shows me how much grit you are capable of. Let's talk about how you could draw on that skill when faced with math challenges.*

Recognition of effort when growth is slow: *Gerald, you stayed with this assignment from beginning to end. Your notes were thorough, and you participated in our discussion. You didn't quite hit the learning target, but you came close, and if you keep up your effort, you're going to start hitting the targets, and even surpassing them.*

Recognition of effort when progress is thwarted: *Alan, I appreciate your effort to contribute to your group's project, even though you joined late. Even if your piece doesn't become part of the final product, you have learned something by jumping into the process.*

Reinforce your commitment to the student and to the Social Contract: *Jackie, I'll never give up on you. I know you can learn and grow. I'll always be in your corner. I'll never give up on enforcing our Social Contract, either. Let's come up with a plan that gives you a chance to grow.*

Demonstrate flexibility as you plan together: *Jim, it seems neither taking breaks nor losing privileges is helping you get hold of yourself. It doesn't matter to me how we work together to get you back on track; I just want to find something that works for you. How would you like to be redirected?*

Share personal stories of growth: *Jeanine, lately you've been looking tired and unmotivated, like you don't have a lot of energy. It happens to me, too. There are days when I come to work tired because the baby was up all night, or I had a cold and couldn't sleep. So I've been there, and I think I know how you feel. Over the years, I've learned to fight through the fatigue and get things done anyway. If I don't, who will? Well, it's the same for you...we all go through times like that. When it happens to you, I suggest you hang in there, even though it's not easy: participate, work extra hard to stay engaged and on the right track. When you do, you'll find the progress you make to be extra satisfying.*

Actions that encourage a growth mindset

Teach students about the characteristics of a growth mindset:

- believe effort leads to mastery more than talent does
- embrace challenges
- persist in the face of adversity
- welcome criticism and feedback as fodder for growth
- find lessons and inspiration in the success of others
- notice successes, even small ones

Acknowledge a mistake. When you make a mistake in front of students, acknowledge it out loud specifically, neither minimizing nor exaggerating the error, and share with students your thought process for fixing it. When appropriate, fix it in the moment. This can powerfully demonstrate how to transform mistakes into learning opportunities.

Share an in-progress learning journey. Perhaps you're learning something outside the classroom: how to cook, or refinish furniture, or play a musical instrument, card game, or sport. Share how you've gotten to your current status: how long it's taken, what some stumbling blocks have been, and how you've overcome them. Talk about what you've accomplished so far, and what you are still struggling with. Finally, talk about your target. Avoid making blanket statements or judgments about your growth; instead, be descriptive and specific.

Share a bad habit or weakness you are currently working to fix. Perhaps you have a notoriously messy desk. Make a point of sharing with students your desire to keep it more orderly. Perhaps invite students to keep a running assessment of your desk. At the end of two weeks, if the data show that it's neater than it was before, celebrate. Or perhaps you say "umm" or "you know" or "like" too much. Have the students keep track of every time you say it. As the number declines, celebrate your growth.

Have students interview someone who habitually does something for the sheer joy of it, rather than to gain status or win something. Discuss how this approach to learning and doing draws on a growth mindset.

Play games that include problem-solving, sustained effort, and self-control. When the group plays together, make winning and losing gracefully a rule. Connect the ability to recover quickly from the disappointment of losing a game to real-life examples of recovery. *Contractors frequently lose bids on projects. They have to make adjustments and keep working. Eventually, they land a bid.*

Share examples of famous people who had or have growth mindsets: *J.K. Rowling was rejected by twelve publishers before one decided to take a chance on her first Harry Potter story. Walt Disney was told to "lose the mouse" because no one would like it.*

Share a list of Abraham Lincoln's failures:[4]

Lost job, 1832

Defeated for legislature, 1832

Failed in business, 1833

Sweetheart (Ann Rutledge) died, 1835

Had nervous breakdown, 1836

Defeated for Speaker, 1838

Defeated for nomination for Congress, 1843

Lost renomination for Congress, 1848

Rejected for Land Officer, 1849

Defeated for Senate, 1854

Defeated for nomination for Vice President, 1856

Again defeated for Senate, 1858

Success! Elected President, 1860

Use the Loop, especially when a task doesn't go as well as you had hoped. Identify what needs improving and how to improve it.

Strategies for Nurturing Your Growth Mindset

Analyze your own tendencies, compared to the teacher growth mindset characteristics detailed above, to develop self-awareness.

Challenge yourself to grow in a nonprofessional area first (e.g., learn a new song to sing, drink eight glasses of water a day). Apply some of the "actions to encourage a growth mindset" detailed above. Here is a summary:

Believe you can do it

Embrace challenges

Put forth sustained effort

Seek feedback/criticism and respond to it

Seek inspiration provided by others who have experienced success in the same area

Notice the results you are getting. Keep track of even small successes.

Next, challenge yourself to grow in a professional area (e.g., seek out a shy student for conversation twice a week). Apply some of the "actions to encourage a growth mindset."

When you are making a split-second decision about which redirection strategy to use with a student, ask yourself: *Which one would best help her grow?* This could also apply to many other areas of teacher decision-making.

ACTION MINDSET

Teaching so that every student can and will grow requires conscious commitment: a declaration to continue patiently trying when solutions are not apparent and attempts fail, even in the face of pushback and our own distaste. It requires a firm determination to build a pathway to success for even those students whose capacities and good qualities are hard to see. The payoff is results instead of reasons why not.

Lawrence wasn't easy for me to deal with. He didn't like being held accountable for his work, and I had high expectations for my students. We made agreements, but he broke them. He was very competitive and had an irritating way of pointing out the mistakes of others. He always had an edge, wanted an advantage, and had never had anyone demand his personal best, so his habits were bad. To be honest, I just wasn't attracted to him. One day I faced the fact that I was holding back on one of my students, and if I didn't help him more, he was probably not going to do well. I decided I needed to know more about him, so I called his dad, and he invited me for a meal. I got a picture of my student's life at home, and saw that he spent a lot of time alone with no adult to help him with his homework. I set it up that 2 or 3 days a week he stayed in the room with me to eat lunch and do his homework. When we began to spend that time together, he became more attractive to me and his work improved.

—middle-level teacher

Who's Responsible for Our Students' Education?

The most productive answer to this important question is: "They are. Their parents are. We are." We each play a part, but the paradox is that we will each be most successful if we act as if it were all up to us. As teachers, we have to consistently create openings for students and their families to take responsibility for their part. Often this is not easy.

It's the beginning, but not enough, to *believe* that we are responsible. Commitment calls for us to *actively provide* the relationship and assistance needed for every student to move along his or her journey of growth, even if it means going outside our comfort zone. Some students may need something special that we cannot provide; even so, we work to identify what is needed and initiate action.

Acting on a commitment to teach each student the skills he needs to develop socially and emotionally and become responsibly independent requires strength and stamina. Moving students in the right direction is sometimes an act of great will, requiring us to tap into our personal reservoir of determination and courage.

Urgency Boosts Action

It also takes diligence and energy to give attention to the many, many details that are part of excellence in teaching, and never just let things go. As every teacher knows, the switch is on from the moment you come into the building to the moment you leave. Whether released or restrained by fear, feeling courageous or doubtful and tired, we must act decisively for the good of our students. Some call this quality of action "moral agency," forwarding others according to our highest moral commitments. One *Developmental Designs* practitioner describes this force within as "urgency."

I have no choice, really. I must do what I can, right now, to get this child straightened out and flying right. The way I see it is that students are learning all the time, for better or worse, and my sense of how urgently important it is for them to grow pushes me to act to keep their learning positive and within my design.

—Fifth grade teacher

Balance patience and impatience

A sense of urgency can call for both patience and impatience in teaching. Impatience is called for in the face of anything that stands between our students and their optimal learning—including student misbehavior, staff dysfunction, preconceived beliefs of others (or your own) about what individual students or groups of students are capable of, district policy barriers, physical plant issues, etc. The urgent stand is: We must put everything we've got into teaching our students, and we don't have time to waste!

Patience may seem an unlikely partner to urgency. Can someone be urgently patient? Yes, when we take time to teach, model, practice, set rules, provide examples, create norms together, seek student endorsement through sharing personal experiences, ask open-ended questions, and work with students who need extra time or special arrangements to develop appropriate behavior or acquire certain skills. Change is hard—it can be slow, incremental, with false starts, peaks and valleys—and internalized social skills are usually hard-won. They develop with patient, committed teaching.

Action-minded Teachers

Consider these ideas for maintaining an action mindset:

- hold the line for adolescents, many of whom test the limits
- act equitably so that everyone can feel supported and can learn
- consistently help students develop their social, emotional, and academic skills, and intervene when they slip
- try strategies outside of their comfort zone when they believe the strategies are good for students
- recognize and work on their professional weak spots
- admit mistakes, fix them, and move on
- slow down and get things right rather than rush ahead and pick up the pieces later
- cultivate student independence through gradually increasing their responsibility

Results of an Action Mindset

Goal setting

The teacher keeps the targets for learning in front of herself and the student so both can note progress and watch for work that still needs to be done to meet the goal. Students learn to self-assess and self-advocate.

Advisory

Someone—teacher or students or both—puts effort into planning each advisory meeting so it builds community, provides a fun start for the day, leverages learning about each other, and provides opportunities for thinking, speaking, listening, and using social skills that help ensure school and life success. Effort put into the meetings pays off in social, emotional, and academic growth. Students and teachers all participate and grow a positive community.

Formative modeling

Teachers and students take time to practice classroom and school routines so that everyone gets the most out of them. The response to classroom disruptions does not rely only on corrective discipline, but includes actions to rebuild the routines in order to head off future disruptions. Gradually, students become responsibly independent.

Empowering language

Teachers take the time and make the effort to talk with students in ways that minimize conflict and maximize school connectedness. As a result, students gradually develop self-control, intrinsic motivation, and resilience.

Effective Pathways to Self-control

Do not let small things build up and do not correct only the most obvious rule-breakers. Take equitable action in response to all infractions by all students, none excepted. This way, students learn to fix their small mistakes, stay on track, and increase their resilience.

Warning Signs

When we respond to small problems, they do not build into major issues in the classroom. Teaching and learning benefit when a teacher habitually moves into action when students lose sight of their goals, or show disinterest and low participation in advisory or in class hours, or consistently mess up routines. These are warning signs, and neither our own fatigue nor student resistance thwart our action mindsets.

Strategies for Nurturing Your Active Mindset

A *Developmental Designs* slogan is "sweat the small stuff." This means take action to provide students with the interventions they need to grow, before and after academic and social difficulties. Operating from an action mindset, here are some ways teachers can consistently sweat the small stuff:

- Set clear expectations before activities to head off potential disruptions.
- Intervene right away when misbehavior begins, so the student can turn it around more easily. Take just a split second to think about which redirect might work best in the situation, with that particular student. Be decisive.

- Have a quick conference with a student you think might need extra support, before he or she slips academically or socially.

- Have a quick conference with a student as soon as you see a pattern of misbehavior or academic difficulty.

- Provide high-achieving students with assignment extensions that engage and challenge them.

Taking actions necessary to help students grow can be exhausting in the moment, but we rest more easily at the end of the day knowing that we took steps necessary to set up and maintain successful student behavior, and we reap the reward in positive student growth.

Develop a sense of urgency. Be decisive and take action. *I need to take care of this now so we can make progress.* A good rule of thumb for action: if you feel unsure about how to intervene—if you lack clarity about what to do—err on the side of intervening in a decisive way.

Sample scenario: It's early in the year. A student publicly insults another student or you. You're not sure whether to just say her name, use a non-verbal cue, use Take a break or TAB Out. What should you do? Take action. Be decisive. Taking clear, decisive action is important. The perpetrator is likely testing you, and others are watching to see if you will take action to restore order. When the stakes are high, an action mindset really helps.

Sample scenario: It's silent, independent work time. Two students start whispering to each other, and their body language indicates they are off topic, perhaps discussing something social in nature. If you let it go, in hopes that they stop, what effect will this have on everyone else? If, on the other hand, you subtly redirect the two, what effect will this have? Redirecting the rule breaking is the way to go: it communicates an equitable, consistent response to rule breaking. Students take note that you will protect the community.

An action mindset helps avoid six common traps:

1. I know I should model this, but I can't afford to spend the time.

2. They should already know how to do this (line up, listen, take notes, hand in papers, raise their hands, etc.)! I'm not going to model it.

3. I know a circle seating format is best for building community, but it's hard to make a circle with the space/furniture limitations, so I'm going to abandon the circle seating format.

4. I know a signal for attention works best when I keep working at it consistently, but the constant vigilance is exhausting, so I'm not using the signal anymore.

5. If I redirect him/her, it will damage our relationship. I'll try other methods, or ignore the behavior.

6. If I redirect him/her, a power struggle will ensue. I'll try other methods, or ignore the behavior.

For each of these, *taking action* is the right thing to do.

1. True, time is valuable, but an ounce of prevention is worth a pound of cure. The few minutes it takes to set a solid expectation for listening is time well spent.

2. Indeed, seventh graders (or first graders, for that matter) *should* know how to raise hands and wait patiently to speak, but *does* everyone actually know how? And, of those who do know how to do it, **will they actually do it** if you don't set the expectation clearly?

3. There are obstacles to circle seating arrangements, but the benefits are important. Make it happen quickly and efficiently, with every student helping.

4. It takes work to maintain the signal for attention, but it's well worth it. Student learning, teacher job satisfaction, and relationships flourish when everyone works together to quickly create silent attention.

5. True, redirecting any student can meet with resistance; it is unrealistic to expect a student to immediately feel grateful! But it is what students need from us, and it will actually improve your teacher-student relationships over time.

6. Some students are bound to push back, and a test of your power may ensue. Stay firm, stay neutral, and avoid getting sucked into a public debate. Think of it this way: if you don't redirect a student who breaks a rule and is a known power-struggler, who has the power?

Avoid making assumptions about students. Instead, tap into your action mindset, and set expectations. Ignoring a rule-breaking behavior opens a Pandora's box of unpleasant surprises. Instead, tap into your action mindset and redirect quickly.

OBJECTIVE MINDSET

When we think of bad days at school, what usually comes to mind are days when something pushed us at least momentarily to drop our professional objectivity and react with strong emotions rather than a balance between concerned interest and objective distance. Professional objectivity is part of the equipment necessary for effective teaching. For example, although we have the power to punish, the challenge each day is to use our best judgment and cool heads to figure out ways to empower students to learn even when they aren't drawn to learning, and to discipline themselves rather than always needing to be directed by adults. On our good days, any accusations or attitudes tossed our way are superseded by our determination to help a student become responsibly independent and academically successful.

There were many days when I found Dante waiting for me in the office, having been referred from class for repeated off-task or disruptive behavior. He was all about cool and seemed to come to school to be admired by his friends and by the girls who thought he was dangerously attractive. It was infuriating that, after a significant intervention (maybe a conference, a plan for fixing the issue, a new seat in the classroom, a call to Mom, etc.)the next morning, or even in the afternoon, he would be back at his game involving maximizing time in the hall, minimizing time on task, and basically skirting school responsibilities.

I could probably count my interventions with Dante in dozens. I remember the many times that, after I was definitely onto his escape artistry, and could definitely have pulled out my hair or blown up at him, I would instead ascertain the reason for his not being in class, remind him of the purpose of our work together and of my belief that he would be able to graduate from high school, and then calmly and quietly walk him up to class where I would find an empty desk near him and model engagement in the class while I made sure that he was (as he usually was) able to re-engage and salvage the last of the class period.

I knew that my only chance with Dante was not with blame or punishment, but to establish over and over again the context for our work together and my faith in him to the point where he grew into it.

—Principal of eighth grade student

Researcher Robert Marzano defines emotional objectivity as part of the necessary mindset of effective disciplinarians: "[A]n effective classroom manager implements and enforces rules and procedures, executes disciplinary actions, and cultivates effective relationships with students without interpreting violations of classroom rules and procedures, negative reactions to disciplinary actions, or lack of response to teacher's attempts to forge relationships as a personal attack."[5]

Max van Manen, in *The Tone of Teaching,* reminds us that "The teacher serves the child by observing from very close proximity while still maintaining distance."[6]

When we lose sight of the individual student, our chances of making a difference in his life are greatly reduced. By connecting to the individual that we can figure out what to say, do, and ask of the student, given his needs, his current skills, and his style of being, including his culture. But it is by remaining enough apart that we can look clearly at the student without the fog of hurt, anger, or culturally-biased tendencies.

Objective-minded Teachers

Consider these ideas for maintaining an objective mindset:

- Avoid personalizing relationship issues, behavior management, and lesson design. Proactive and reactive moves are made with neutrality.

- Use the collaboratively-made Social Contract as a way of changing the voice of authority.

- Use neutral methods even when the urge to express emotion is high. For example, a teacher who is used to getting her students' attention by yelling "Listen up!" or "Can I have your attention!" uses the signal for attention until the signal becomes second nature to her.

- Separate *who the student is* from *what she does.*

- Create a "Student Profile" to hold onto a positive vision for each student, especially when the details of the present moment are discouraging.

- Remain neutral when students are doing well *and* when they are not. The exception: passion about content is inspiring to students and important to model.

- Mentally refer to student needs, developmental realities, culture, personality, and assets when planning for *all* students' success, especially those who are struggling academically and/or socially/emotionally.

- Develop a sense of when to swim against the current and when to go with it.

- Create a "self-profile" to identify cultural or temperamental qualities that may influence challenging work with students.

Example: a certain class is chattier than most. Rather than allow this to irritate him, the teacher figures out ways to build in extra turn-and-talks during lecture time and longer cooperative learning times, but insists on quiet, focused listening when he addresses the whole group and when students share their projects with the whole group.

Payoffs of an Objective Mindset

Goal setting

The teacher and student work as partners to set learning targets in such a way that a student's goals authentically reflect what he wants for himself, as well as what the teacher and his family want for him. As a result, the student learns to self-reflect, self-assess, and self-advocate.

Advisory

Teachers remain objective about what their students need and want at any particular time, taking into consideration that sometimes following student preferences might be the best way for them to grow; other times, following student preferences could lead to a lack of growth, because people can get into ruts. As a result, students' needs for autonomy, competence, relationship, and fun are met. Students grow important social-emotional skills, such as tolerance, appreciation, self-control, and assertion.

Formative modeling

An objective look at student misbehavior may sometimes reveal that what is needed is more modeling and practicing of routines or some one-to-one conferencing, not more corrective discipline. The opposite could be true, too, and remaining objective enables us to decide on the appropriate course of action. When we objectively match the support to the student need, students are more likely to grow.

Empowering language

Responding to student attitudes and behavior demands a cool head, objectivity that prevents verbal responses that we later regret. When we manage misbehavior without showing students that we are upset, we are the rock-solid, confident, undeterred adults they need us to be in order to grow.

Effective Pathways to Self-control

Sometimes the causes of misbehavior have to do with our lack of clarity in directions, or rushing through demonstrations, not checking for understanding, or ignoring students' need for fun, rather than simple contrariness on the part of students. When our objective analysis indicates that redirection needs to be replaced with proactive supports and clarifications, a more peaceful, productive classroom emerges.

Warning Signs

It's easy to tell when our objectivity slips: we feel miserable. We find ourselves irritated by student behaviors, impatient with students who don't or won't follow directions, hurt by confrontations. Taking a break, talking with a kind colleague, even distracting ourselves by jotting down a shopping list for after school may give us the space we need to recollect ourselves, regain objectivity, and refocus on teaching and learning.

Strategies for Nurturing Your Objective Mindset

Take a curious stance about students, even when you are faced with sustained difficulty or high emotion. For example, if a student consistently pushes back against your redirection, reflect on moments when the student is collaborative with you or with other students. Adjust your picture of him to include a variety of qualities, then address the situation from that stance.

Keep revitalized. If you are not taking care of yourself, remaining objective in the face of constant demands can be extremely difficult. Here are some revitalization techniques:

In the moment: Keep water handy, and pause at the first sign of losing objectivity for a quick, soothing drink. Try taking a couple of deep, slow breaths, or centering your emotions in some other way. For example, if a student with anger issues loses control and snaps at you, remind yourself: *Stay calm: it probably has nothing to do with me; when he's calm, we'll discuss what just happened and how we'll fix it. In the meantime, I'll calmly send him to our break spot and get back to teaching.*

Develop a neutralizing mantra. Create a short phrase to support a level response in challenging situations:

It's not about me.

Breathe, breathe.

All students want to grow.

Little spaces in the school day—as students are passing, at lunch, during your prep period: Exchange a pleasant word or two with a colleague. A moment at your desk with your eyes closed can do wonders, as can a cup of tea, coffee, or juice. Movement and fresh air can also keep you centered: a brief walk around school grounds might help.

Weekends: Make sure to take at least one day completely off from grading papers and planning lessons. Get away from it all and refresh yourself in a way that fits your needs. This might mean a long nap, or plenty of exercise, or an excursion to a nearby park or town.

---

1 Parker Palmer, *The Courage to Teach* (San Francisco: Jossey-Bass, 1998), 2.

2 Lisa S. Blackwell, Kali H. Trzesniewski, and Carol Sorich Dweck, "Implicit Theories of Intelligence Predict Achievement across an Adolescent Transition: A Longitudinal Study and Intervention," *Child Development* 78, no. 1 (2007): 246-263.

3 Carol S. Dweck, "The Perils and Promises of Praise," *Educational Leadership* 65, no. 2 (October 2007): 35.

4 Adapted from *The Little Book of Big Motivational Quotes* by Sid Savara, http://sidsavara.com/wp-content/uploads/2009/09/little-book-of-big-motivational-quotes-sidsavara-com.pdf

5 Robert J. Marzano, *Classroom Management that Works: Research-Based Strategies for Every Teacher* (Alexandria, VA: Association for Supervision and Curriculum Development, 2003), 68.

6 Max van Manen, *The Tone of Teaching* (Ontario: Althouse, 2003), 26-28.

CHAPTER THREE

Advisory

REFLECTING ON ADVISORY

BARRIERS TO ADVISORY

STRATEGIES FOR ADVISORY

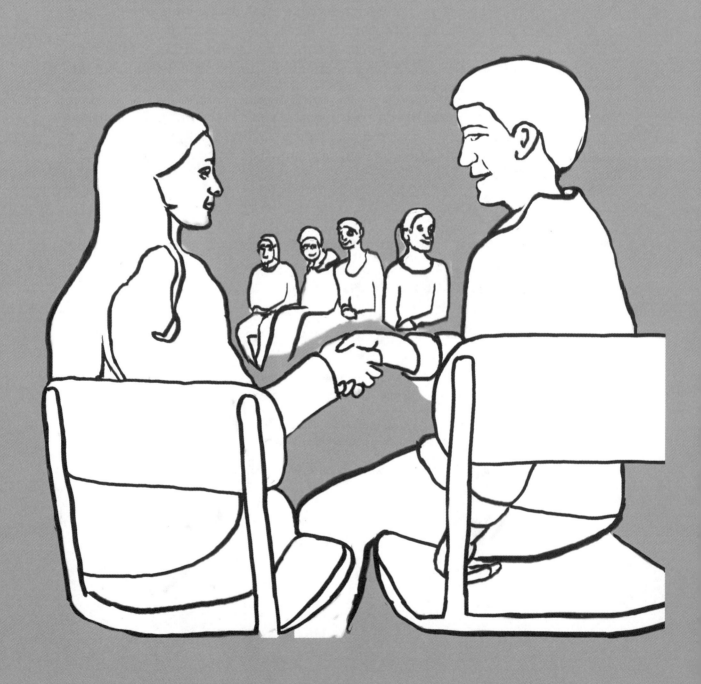

REFLECTING ON ADVISORY

Activate your growth mindset as you consider this vision for a safe and engaged advisory community. Reflect on the degree to which you engage best practices in advisory. Even in the strongest practice, there is always room for growth. Even in a beginning practice, there is always evidence of strength. Take stock, then select what you want to work on.

General Practice

1. **Space:** Are all students gathered comfortably in a circle, without obstructions?

2. **Length/content:** Does the meeting last 15 to 20 minutes and include all components in the right order?

3. **Teacher participation:** Do I sit in the circle and participate with the students in all components?

4. **Creating endorsement:** Do I teach students the importance of our CPR and A+ meetings, including each component, and help them make connections to their lives outside of school?

5. **Transition to advisory:** Do all students join the circle on time, quietly, empty-handed, and with minimal reminding?

6. **School support:** Do all students arrive on time and remain in the room for the duration of advisory?

7. **Modeling:** Introducing a new format or activity, do I model the essential behaviors or procedures and give students an opportunity to practice?

8. **The Loop:** Do I use the Loop to assess learning, to reflect broadly, and to plan for success?

9. **Pathways to Self-control:** Do I use a variety of redirection tools to ensure that each student is learning self-control and moving toward responsible independence?

Circle of Power and Respect: Greeting

10. **Content:** Do I plan greetings appropriate to students' age, development, level of social skills, interests, and the time of year?

11. **Eye contact:** Do all students make eye contact?

12. **Speaking and Listening:** Do all students use respectful voices and body language?

13. **Participation:** Does each student and adult greet and receive a greeting from at least one other person?

14. **Audience:** Do all students watch, listen to, and honor the greetings that are passed around the circle?

Circle of Power and Respect: Sharing

15. **Relationship building:** Do I use a variety of formats (including interactive sharing) and topics to deepen sharing skills and relationships among group members?

16. **Sharer participation:** Are all students eager or at least willing to share during CPR?

17. **Sharer content:** Do all students share appropriate information, especially during interactive sharing, so that others get to know them better?

18. **Sharer speaking skills:** Do all sharers speak in strong, audible voices?

19. **Audience during interactive sharing:** Do all students ask questions that are respectful and open-ended (elicit detail) and help students get to know each other?

20. **Audience listening:** Do all students listen attentively to each sharer and to all questions and comments?

Circle of Power and Respect: Activity

21. **Content:** Do I plan activities appropriate for students' development, levels of social skills, interests, need for movement, readiness for challenge, and the time of year?

22. **Student participation:** Do all students smile and interact in cooperative and respectful ways?

23. **Student problem-solving skills:** Do all students demonstrate problem-solving skills in social dilemmas and/or games?

Circle of Power and Respect: Daily News

24. **Interactive content:** Do all students contribute ideas to the news message in various ways?

25. **Purposeful content:** Do I include a variety of useful information for students in the message, including vocabulary building and other connections to academic content?

26. **Interaction with the news:** Before CPR, do all students read the daily news and follow the message directions with little prompting?

27. **Reading news aloud:** At the end of the CPR meeting, do all students read aloud and actively listen to the daily news?

Circle of Power and Respect: Student-led CPR

28. **Planning:** Do I provide a planning template to students and feedback on their plan in advance to prepare to lead CPR?

29. **Reflection:** Do I (or a student) facilitate reflection on what went well and what needs to change next time?

30. **Student participation:** Do students frequently take on CPR leadership with enthusiasm?

Activity Plus

31. **Daily news:** Do my daily news messages inform students of meetings' contents?

32. **Activity:** Do I share expectations with students and structure the activity to maximize student productivity?

33. **Greeting:** Do all students briefly and respectfully greet each other?

34. **Reflection:** At the close of an A+, do I pose open-ended questions that invite students to reflect on the activity?

BARRIERS TO ADVISORY

1. Identify barriers

What gets in the way in your advisory? Review what other teachers identify as barriers to growth in advisory. Keeping in mind the advisory element you've selected to work on, identify the common barriers to growth that fit your experience.

2. Identify strategy areas

The barriers are grouped into the six strategy areas: Relationship, Teacher Preparation, Expectations, Accountability, Endorsement, and Engagement. Identify the strategy area most relevant to your experience. For example, if barriers described under Accountability reflect what you observe in students or yourself, start by reading that Strategies section on page 53.

Common Barriers to Growth

Relationship

Students do not like or want to be in a circle with each other.

Students are impatient with the process.

Students are not comfortable asking open-ended questions.

There is a low level of trust among students; they may not feel safe enough to participate.

Students are not willing or eager to participate.

Students don't respond constructively to my redirection.

I am concerned that upholding the expectations of this process or component will harm our relationships or will anger or alienate students.

Teacher Preparation

The room arrangement and/or size does not allow for a meeting circle and/or for activities.

Our schedule, announcements, late buses, breakfast, Pledge of Allegiance, or other interruptions don't allow for a full meeting, or they disrupt attendance.

Time considerations and student skill levels limit my selection of greetings, shares, and/or activities.

Greetings, shares, and/or activities are too long, repeat too often, or aren't a good fit for my students.

I have tasks to attend to during advisory that limit my participation.

I'm not always sure about students' social skills and interests.

I need more ideas and planning time (for components, reflections questions, daily news messages, etc.).

I am unclear about or forget the steps of the practice or process or what strategy is best when.

There just isn't enough time!

Expectations

Students take too long to do a routine or a meeting component.

Behavior disruptions often slow down the meeting.

Students do not know, or need reminders about, routines or component expectations.

Students lack the skills to interact cooperatively and respectfully.

Students are unclear about or lack confidence for leading CPR.

Students lack conversation skills and/or confidence.

I have not carefully shifted the responsibility for problem-solving to students.

When I offer students topic choice, I do not check in with them beforehand to catch inappropriate topics.

Accountability

Behavior disruptions often slow down the meeting.

Students know the routine but are not held accountable to expectations.

Students don't respond constructively to my redirection.

Endorsement

Students do not want to be in a circle and/or to come to advisory.

Students resist the modeling and/or set-up steps.

Students don't respond constructively to my redirection.

Students tend to interact positively only with their friends.

A few students seem to sabotage a routine or a meeting component.

Students do not like or see the importance of a routine, meeting component, or meeting leadership.

Students resist setting up the structure; they want to get to the activity itself.

I don't see the value of creating endorsement.

Most students follow the routine, but some need many reminders.

I need more ideas and planning time to develop endorsement for components and routines.

Engagement

Students do not want to come to advisory.

Students are not interested in the topics I select for sharing.

Students do not seem to enjoy activities.

Students know how to but do not buy in to reading and responding to the message.

STRATEGIES FOR ADVISORY

The strategies are organized into six areas: Relationship, Teacher Preparation, Expectations, Accountability, Endorsement, and Engagement. Follow these steps to make the most of the detailed suggestions provided:

1. Read Chapter Two: Mindsets Create the Tone of Teaching as context for all the strategies.
2. Read the strategies areas identified by your review of Barriers to Advisory.
3. Follow suggestions and your interest to read other, related areas.

General resources

Find specific resources are referenced throughout the strategies, e.g., a grid of activities or article about creating endorsement. Explore the following *Developmental Designs* resources for additional, detailed support for advisory:

- *Developmental Designs 1 Resource Book*
- *Developmental Designs 2 Resource Book*
- *The Advisory Book: Building a Community of Learners Grades 5-9*
- *Face to Face Advisories: Bridging Cultural Gaps in Grades 5-9*
- *Classroom Discipline: Guiding Adolescents to Responsible Independence*
- *The Circle of Power and Respect Advisory Meeting DVD*
- *Modeling and Practicing Classroom Routines DVD*
- www.DevelopmentalDesigns.org (free articles, meeting content, and other resources)
- http://www.YouTube.com/user/DevelopmentalDesigns (see practices in action)

RELATIONSHIP

A fundamental *Developmental Designs* principle is that students are more successful when they have strong, positive relationships with their peers and their teachers. Advisory is a time when students and teachers can create, strengthen, refresh, and celebrate their connectedness and prepare for a peaceful, productive school day.

Mindsets are key

All of the components of advisory are designed to strengthen students' relationships with each other and with their teacher. A low level of trust makes students reluctant to take the risk of participating in school. Some may participate minimally, but show little engagement or interest.

Your belief that a strong community can and will develop, no matter what challenges arise, and your leadership to make it happen, are vital. If students are reluctant at times to follow your lead to participate or share in advisory, think about whether your verbal and nonverbal language invites participation. Do you consistently indicate that students' lives are of interest to you? Be clear with students about the fact that their good relationships with each other will help the community, will strengthen their social skills, and will help them succeed in school. See Chapter Two: Mindsets Create the Tone of Teaching, and Endorsement below, pages 59, for strategies.

Is this a group issue or an individual issue?

To assess trust levels in the group, ask:

- Do we need more time and/or support to get to know each other, or does everyone feel comfortable and safe?

- Do certain students dominate the class or otherwise disrupt feelings of safety?

- Has there been an incident recently, in or outside of school, that affects our advisory?

- Do you have unresolved issues with someone in the group?

If the answer to any of these questions is "yes," consider the issue, and read the following suggestions for strengthening relationships in your advisory community.

Build Teacher-student Relationships

Reflect

Reflecting on your relationships with students may reveal needed changes for optimal student growth.

Think of a student you struggle with, and list several of his positive traits. Reflect on how frequently you acknowledge those with him. Does he know you see good in him?

Think of a student you struggle with, and list some of her negative aspects. Write an opposite for each negative characteristic, and think about situations when this student behaves in a positive manner.

Think of a student you often redirect. Reflect on your relationship with him/her. Use the Student Profile in the *Developmental Designs 1 Resource Book*, page 22. Is it generally positive? What do you do to get to know him/her better?

Support relationship by supporting student accountability

Redirecting students and keeping them accountable is hard work, but it is essential, because it protects and encourages them. Build trust with students by showing them that you will be fair and consistent and will keep the classroom safe.

Use the Loop

In connection with an activity, or new greeting or share experience, or whenever you think students might need to reflect and note or plan for improvement ask students:

- How did we do?

- What should we do differently next time?

- What strengths will we retain?

- What do we want to remember about this experience?

Every time you ask students these questions, you check in on their comfort level and you reinforce the community's strengths. Use Loop questions to teach students how to create supportive, safe environments and to show your commitment to the advisory community. You are saying: *How are we doing? Let's make it better!*

Encourage Healthy Peer Relationships

You are the relationship shepherd for your advisory

Students rely on their advisory teacher to teach and assess skills and to set and revise boundaries appropriately for the community of growing adolescents.

Assess the strength of the community: Periodically (every month or six weeks or if a recent change or experience warrants) assess the sense of safety for individuals and for the group. Use a quick visual show of thumbs or "fist of five" at the close of a meeting: *Use a fist of five to show me how comfortable you were with our sharing today, one for not comfortable and five for very comfortable.*

Assess social skills: Use Assessing Social Skills in *The Advisory Book*, page 267, to gauge students' social skills in each component. Help them strengthen their skills with appropriate greeting, sharing, and activities. See *The Advisory Book*, pages 211-215, for a table of meeting content for various needs.

Reinforce the importance of rules and expectations: Using personal stories and drawing connections to students' lives outside of school make clear the essential role that rules and protocols have in creating and maintaining a safe community. See Endorsement below, pages 59, for more about helping students endorse the challenging aspects of advisory meetings.

Greeting hazards and opportunities

The greeting must not be used to convey negative feelings or opinions or to display power. Once students are clear about the expectations, rigorously enforce the standards, and do not overlook small infractions. A seemingly small thing like mumbling or mispronouncing a name damages the connectedness of the group. On the other hand, a special greeting can be a bond among students; for example, the group could create a unique handshake.

Activity hazards and opportunities

Use low-risk activities until you feel students are ready for additional challenge, even if other advisories have moved to greater challenges. Use a quick assessment (fist of five or show of thumbs) after activities to find out which are their favorites. You might be surprised! One sixth grade teacher's group latched on to the nursery-school game A Tisket, a Tasket, altered it to their liking, and returned to it over and over. If you can't find activities that students take on with ease, back up:

- reflect on whether there are specific safety issues (a bullying student, language barriers, etc.), and conference with individuals as needed

- return to conversations about endorsing the activity component; students may need additional rules to feel safe (see below, Endorsement).

Increase the trust challenge when they are ready: A variety of activities are designed to build trust by demanding more cooperation from the group. Indicators of readiness for higher-risk activities include:

- responding appropriately when a student makes a mistake

- self-control to handle movement and physical contact

- trust and respect necessary for competition.

Resources:

- See *Developmental Designs 1 Resource Book*, pages 181-184, for team- and trust-building activities.

- Read how one teacher leveraged his strong CPR community to establish positive connections among diversity in the article *The Circle of Power and Respect: A Weeklong Thematic Focus on Heritage*, by Scott Tyink and Chris Hagedorn, at www.DevelopmentalDesigns.org.

Sharing hazards and opportunities

Start with low-risk sharing topics until the community's relationships can support greater risk. For example, sharing about favorite ice cream flavors requires much less risk than sharing about family experiences. If students share about a personal topic and people laugh, the health of the group will be set back. In a community with strong relationships, students can use sharing to help them heal or get reassurance from their peers. When they are ready, you can choose a topic that asks students for more personal information. Watch carefully when a student shares on a more personal topic, to ensure respectful responses and stop inappropriate ones right away.

If the group is quite introverted, build confidence with low-risk, playful topics until students begin to relax during sharing (evidenced by quick responses, smiles, and familiarity with the routine). Invite a more outgoing student to begin the share for a new format, especially when introducing interactive sharing.

Resource: See *The Advisory Book*, pages 64-72, for more on sequencing sharing according to students' skill levels.

Teach the skill of open-ended questioning: Use an A+ advisory to practice asking and responding to open-ended questions before including them in a share. Be the first sharer when you introduce the interactive format. Choose an interesting topic, then coach the dialogue that follows. You are modeling how to share personal information with confidence, and guiding positive group conduct. Observe the respect and safety students seem to feel; quickly assess if you are not sure. One by one, students will be more likely to take the risk of sharing.

Resource: See *The Advisory Book*, Scaffolding Questioning Skills, page 69, and Appendix F, page 271.

Build inclusion through seating

Pay attention to the seating arrangement. When students always sit next to the same person, they don't get to know everyone. Be direct with students about the community's need for everyone to get to know everyone, at least a little (see Endorsement below). Vary seating arrangements using structures such as clock partners or seating by birthdays: *Sit with your three o'clock partner today. Sit in order of birth dates today, with the earliest birth date in this chair.*

Resource: Use sample A+ advisories and activities in *The Advisory Book* to guide discussions of community issues and social skills. For example, use activity time for a Stop and Think (page 113) or to discuss the "us versus them" dynamic (page 187). See Chapter Three: Activity Plus Advisories, and hundreds of sample A+ meetings on social topics in Chapter Five: 170 Thematic Advisories.

Resource to build relationship across cultures

Examine social and psychological dynamics that tend to push us apart, and identify changes that can pull us together with *Face to Face Advisories*, by Linda Crawford. 125+ meetings, with complete component content provided, prompt development of social skills, critical thinking, and open discussion.

TEACHER PREPARATION

Implementing the four meeting components is just the beginning of great *Developmental Designs* advisories. The more proficient teachers become, the more they include support for student self-management through Pathways, modeling, and the Social Contract; clear and empowering language; getting to know each other; and regular reflection to build understanding and responsible independence (the Loop). If you have participated in *Developmental Designs* workshop training, review the supporting practices and strategies used for CPR and A+ advisories in the *Developmental Designs 1 Resource Book* and the *Developmental Designs 2 Resource Book*.

Mindsets are key

Advisory teachers need to use the three teacher mindsets: growth, action, and objective. For example, planning greeting, share, and activity content requires an action mindset to avoid repeating the same content over and over. When there are divisive tendencies among students, envisioning your advisory group as capable of trust and cooperation requires a growth mindset. Learn more about mindsets and strategies for maintaining them in Chapter Two: Mindsets Create the Tone of Teaching.

Review *your* endorsement

Be sure you fully endorse the rationale for a community-building advisory. Finding time, matching content to skill levels, and other requirements of the practice are much easier when you truly endorse it. Read *The Advisory Book's* rationale and pay-offs for advisory, pages 9-20.

Resource: Read how a Spanish-immersion teacher persisted and developed CPR as "the most vital key to social acceptance and academic learning in my classroom." See the article *Empezamos!*, by Gail Harju, at www.DevelopmentalDesigns.org.

Value of teacher participation

Your participation in advisory is important. If you have been in the habit of using this time for additional preparation or other tasks, reprioritize your advisory to the top. The students need you in the circle, participating and monitoring their behavior; left on their own, many opportunities are lost. See above, Relationship/You are the relationship shepherd for your advisory, page 38, for more about your critical role.

Build student endorsement

Early in the year, have conversations with students about why participation in building a healthy learning community is important, and model and discuss why being good at greeting, sharing, and playing cooperatively are important. Throughout the year you can refresh endorsement proactively or if students seem to be disconnecting from advisory. See below, Endorsement/Finding time to have endorsing conversations, page 60, for preparation ideas.

Value of modeling

The modeling required at the beginning of the year will slow the pace of meetings. However, stories abound of teachers who skipped this crucial step and regretted it by October, because students were not clear about the rules and expectations, and confusion and disruption prevailed. Much more encouraging are the stories of advisory communities that model and practice plenty at the beginning of the year, then function efficiently for the rest of the year. *Go slow to go fast!* Read about how to use modeling efficiently and effectively in Strategies for Modeling and Practicing, below on page 90.

Skillful use of Pathways

Like many aspects of *Developmental Designs*, Pathways to Self-control permeates the school day, including advisory. Students tend to respond calmly and positively to the redirection practices of Pathways. The key is to match the redirection to the student and the situation at hand. If students tend to have strong emotional responses to redirection, carefully observe which ones work best, with the least pushback and repeat misbehavior. Have quick conferences with individual students if you need their input to determine which tools will work best. Read below, Strategies for Pathways to Self-control, page 120, for more suggestions.

Prepare the space

Move furniture as necessary to make a true circle. After modeling and practicing, adolescents can set up the room quickly and restore it after the meeting, and this gross-motor activity helps release energy. Some teachers have their last-period class arrange the circle for the following morning's advisory meeting; others have the first arrivers in the morning create the circle. Still others have the whole group arrange the circle (to create inspiration for this task, see below, Endorsement/Coming to circle, page 63).

If there is not room for a true circle, perhaps you can use a nearby space, sit on the floor, or come up with another solution. If you really are stuck with an oval, make sure students switch their seating daily, so the same students are not always in the out-of-sight places.

Keep students present and focused on advisory

Encourage your staff to avoid scheduling other activities during advisory time. If this must happen from time to time, incorporate the activity into an Activity Plus meeting on those days so students don't miss out on community-building.

If allocated time for advisory is short, request that announcements not be made during advisory or, at the very least, that they be kept brief and timed at the very beginning of advisory, to avoid content interruptions.

In many schools, students with special needs are mainstreamed during advisory time. (In fact, many schools are attracted to the *Developmental Designs* approach because they are looking for ways to make school safer and more inclusive for students needing extra support.) Methods for inclusion vary. One involves spreading students with Emotional/Behavioral Disorders among the regular advisory classrooms and encouraging full participation. They are accompanied in advisory by a supportive paraprofessional, and they return to a pullout program if their behavior requires it.

Deal with latecomers

Some tardiness issues may be beyond your control. Here are some things you can do to minimize problems:

- Look for patterns. As soon as you see a pattern of tardiness, quick-conference with the student, and come up with a plan to fix the problem.

- Alter the timing of your meeting. For example, if you do everything in your power to make sure a bus arrives on time, yet it's always late, maybe delaying the start of the meeting a few minutes would allow riders on that bus to participate fully. That's quite a sacrifice, though—keep working on getting that bus to arrive on time! A similar scenario could apply to students who have breakfast at school.

Find time to plan for advisory

Share the planning. For example, five teachers could each plan one CPR per week, and share the plans with their colleagues. Read *The Advisory Book*, Chapter Four: Planning Advisories, for team planning suggestions and sample planning structures.

Sort the free greeting, share, and activity descriptions at www.DevelopmentalDesigns.org by community level and other characteristics, then plan meetings for your group.

File your meeting plans and reuse them next year. As time goes by, you'll need much less planning time.

Use *The Advisory Book* and *Face to Face Advisories*

Save time by using the advisories in *The Advisory Book*. It has detailed outlines for over one hundred advisories, thematically organized. You may choose from hundreds of activities, greetings, and sharing topics, all with risk levels and other characteristics indicated. *Face to Face Advisories* outlines 125+ cultural conversations that build appreciation for diversity and foster action for equity.

Plan Appropriate Content

Match content to skill level

Your plans for meetings will depend on your students' levels of social skills and on the strength of the community. When you use pre-planned advisories, consider whether you need to make adjustments, such as extra support for some individuals (see below, Expectations/When clear expectations aren't enough, page 49). For support with assessment of social skills, see *The Advisory Book*, pages 267-269.

Once you have a clear idea of students' skills, you can select meeting content that is a good match, avoiding confusion and frustration. As students grow in their social skills, you can increase the complexity of activities so they continue to grow.

Resources:

- Read *The Advisory Book* sections on sequencing component content:

    Sequencing greeting content, pages 53-56

    Sequencing sharing content, pages 64-72

    Sequencing activity content, pages 78-82

- Read about school's assessment of student CPR experiences in the article Query Students about CPR, by Melanie Poulliot, at www. DevelopmentalDesigns.org.

Match content to your group using the content-type and community-level indicators in the following:

- *The Advisory Book*: use the grid on pages 211-215 to find the right greetings, share formats, and activities, and the Table of Contents to find what you need among the CPR and A+ sample advisories

- www.DevelopmentalDesigns.org: greeting, share, and game instructions are identified by community level

- *Developmental Designs 1 Resource Book*: see the activity grid on pages 174-175

- *Tried and True Classroom Games and Greetings:* favorite activities of experienced *Developmental Designs* practitioners

Aim for interactive sharing: Use an action mindset to make sure students gain the skills necessary for interactive sharing. Without this format, sharing (and the community) remains limited by students' lack of certain skills. See Expectations/Support interactive sharing, page 51, for more about preparing the group for interactive sharing.

Choose good component combinations

Prepare for your meetings by choosing components that complement each other in their time requirements. It's all right to occasionally combine or skip a meeting component. Most components take longer the first few times you use them; plan accordingly.

Examples:

- If you choose a longer activity, plan a quick whip share instead of a longer share format, such as interactive share.

- If you know sharing will take longer than usual, choose an active greeting and skip the activity.

- Use the A+ format for advisory if you know the activity will take longer than ten minutes or you want to build more reflection into the process.

Plan reflection using the Loop

If you and your students do not use the Loop for reflection and planning, you're in for a pleasant surprise. The Loop enhances learning by teaching students to organize their thinking; to become more conscious of and articulate about what they experience; to assess their own work; and to plan for continuous progress.

To begin using the Loop in your CPR process, choose three consecutive CPR meetings in which you will begin to use it. Look at the greeting, share, and activity content you have planned for each meeting, and write down two planning and two reflection questions you will ask students about each of these components. During the meetings, ask the Loop questions and field student responses. Notice how the students begin to consider successful actions before and after they do them.

Resources:

Developmental Designs 1 Resource Book, page 5

The Advisory Book, page 36

Creating Effective Daily News Messages

The daily news messages included in *The Advisory Book's* advisories (see Chapter Five: 170 Thematic Advisories) are examples of good message content, depth, and format.

Stay clear about the purpose of the message

The summary below and *The Advisory Book,* pages 38-39, enumerate benefits of regular use of the daily news message. Keep in mind the three main purposes of the message as you plan it:

- **Review the day:** Students are able to responsibly and independently find out what's going on at school that day

- **Provide post-activity transition:** Reading the chart together at the end of the meeting helps everyone settle down after an activity

- **Prime academic skills:** Students practice academic and writing skills and build their vocabularies.

Choose a good place and process for the message

Choose a place in the room where several students can simultaneously stand before the message, read it, and respond before the meeting begins. Have several markers handy for written interaction. Model and practice with students how to enter the advisory space, walk to the message right away, and interact with it before taking a seat in the circle. If the message isn't already in the circle, move it to a space between two chairs just before the meeting begins.

Establish a message-making routine

Some teachers complete tomorrow's daily news message before they leave school in the evening; others do it in the morning. Choose a routine that works for you. *Do not change the order of the components* of CPR—for example, reading the daily news aloud at the start of the meeting. If time is short, hold each student accountable for reading the message individually before the meeting begins, and appoint one or two students each day to read the message aloud to the group at the end of the meeting. Plan the meeting so you have a minute or two at the end to settle down and read the message together.

Resources:

- Read how one teacher saved time and increased interaction with PowerPoint daily news messages: *Using Technology to Support CPR,* by Nancy Curl, at www.DevelopmentalDesigns.org.

- See *The Advisory Book,* pages 83-88, for more about reading the news.

Student-led CPRs

Eventually, students can and should lead components of CPRs, and finally entire meetings. Tell them this at the beginning of the year to increase their interest in advisory (see below, Endorsement, pages 59, for more ideas). When you see that students have the skills required to lead a component, conference with them to develop a plan for them to do so. Eventually, all students will have this leadership opportunity.

Student-led CPR resources

- Find student planning and reflection sheets on pages 48-49 in the *Developmental Designs 1 Resource Book*

- Find detailed support for preparing students to lead CPR in *The Advisory Book,* pages 89-97.

- See a summary of two teachers' process of guiding students to lead CPR in the article *Student-led Circle of Power and Respect,* by Erin Klug, at www.DevelopmentalDesigns.org

- Read how one teacher carefully develops leadership skills in *Pass the Torch without Anyone Getting Burned,* by Eric Charlesworth, at www.DevelopmentalDesigns.org.

Efficient student-led CPRs

Student-led CPRs shouldn't take any longer than teacher-led ones. Thorough planning is the key to well-paced, engaging meetings. If necessary, you can tactfully move things along.

Activity Plus

Tips for common challenges to a successful A+ meeting:

- Use simultaneous greeting, i.e. greetings in which partners or triads greet all at once. These greetings can take a minute or less, leaving more time for the share or activity. See *The Advisory Book,* pages 211-212, for a grid that identifies quick greetings.

- How to structure the extended activity time? Use the structures suggested in Chapter Three, or use one of the dozens of pre-planned A+ advisories in Chapter Five in *The Advisory Book.*

- When to use an extended activity? Browse the pages of *The Advisory Book* dedicated to A+ activities and sample advisories to get a sense of what types of activities are likely to need more time than what is available in the CPR format. A+ is perfect for a longer game or when you use a structure such as a Stop and Think or a planning meeting.

- Remember that reflection question can focus on either the process or the content of the meeting. Try these starters:

How well did you...

What did you enjoy most about...

What is one thing you learned from...

See *The Advisory Book* for sample reflection questions, pages 101 and 272, and sample A+ daily news messages, pages 136-208.

EXPECTATIONS

Often, students do not rise to teacher expectations because they are not clear about them.

Is this a group or an individual issue?

Take notes for a few days about which students are having difficulty following expectations and seem unclear about a routine. As you look through the following support strategies, keep your notes in mind. Some strategies are ideal when the whole group needs clarification about or practice with expectations; other strategies serve better when just one or two students need review.

Review *your* endorsement of setting expectations

Making sure everyone is clear about your expectations takes some time, but you regain that time and more as classroom routines proceed smoothly. The tone and productivity of the classroom improve with less reminding and redirecting. Read *Classroom Discipline*, Chapter Five, about the rationale and benefits of modeling and practicing and about other ways to prime for learning.

Model routines

Use modeling and practicing to introduce a new greeting, sharing format, or activity. Remodel as needed the first few times you use the new component until students clearly know how to do it. *Then stop remodeling and hold the group accountable.*

Balance modeling and redirection: Don't get caught in an endless cycle of remodeling and reminding. Once everyone is clear about an expectation, hold everyone accountable. Have a quick or full conference with any student who doesn't adhere to the routine, and come up with a plan to fix the problem. The student might need extra support, or could be testing you, or may have some other issue. Conferencing should surface the problem and create a plan for improvement.

On the other hand, if you find your redirections do not result in adjusted behavior of quite a few students, expectations may need to be clarified. Try checking for understanding just before the start of a component, then model and practice to resolve confusion.

Use visuals to support expectations: Early in the year, create with the group a visual reminder of expectations for effective greetings, shares, and activities. Create another one for the audience's role during meetings. Display and refer to them to keep expectations clear. Take them down when you no longer need to refer to them, and repost them when you think students need a reminder. Once they have served their purpose, remove them again so they don't become stale.

Set redirection expectations

Have you set clear expectations for how students are to respond to teacher redirection? If you have not, do so. Be sure all students are clear that their response to redirection must be quiet and immediate. Discuss this with the group, and ask for endorsement:

There will be times during our CPR when you do not understand why I am redirecting you. I get that, and I understand that it's not fun to get called out by your teacher. Respond to the redirect, and get right back on track, without arguing, negotiating, or complaining. Our focus is on our greeting, share, or game. If we stop when someone messes up, we'll get bogged down. Follow the redirect quickly and quietly, and later, if you or I feel we should communicate, we can do so. Is everyone OK with this?

This part of expectation-setting is crucial. It proactively makes clear how to deal with disagreement about redirection, and promises resolution of the disagreement.

Keep the Contract alive

Help students see the connection between their own behavior and the Social Contract you created together. Use a think-aloud to model analyzing how behavior did or did not follow the Contract:

Mr. Filkins just told me I need to pay attention to Samara's share. Let's see…our Social Contract says be respectful and participate actively. I guess staring out the window wasn't respectful, and I wasn't listening actively, or at least I wasn't showing Samara that I was. I'll just turn around in my seat, face her, and show her some respect.

Reinforce and teach with the Loop

Use the Loop before and after each greeting, share, and activity to provide students with a chance to create and maintain group expectations for CPR meetings. Use the Loop until everyone successfully hits the target with a new greeting, share, or activity, then reduce your use of the Loop, and be sure to *hold the group accountable*. Return to modeling and explicit use of the Loop whenever it appears that students need a reminder, or when you are beginning a more challenging greeting, share, or activity.

When clear expectations aren't enough

Some students may need extra mediators and support to know what to do and how to do it. They've seen the modeling, they've helped create the written reminders and have referred to them, they've participated in the Loop, but things still aren't going right. Have a quick conference with each of these students ASAP. The plan you devise in the conference could take many forms. For example, if a student can't seem to refrain from blurting, you might:

• allow him a pen, paper, and clipboard during meetings to write down his comments

• have the student sit next to you during meetings

• coach the student to quietly tap her fingers on her knees during the meeting to mitigate what may be a sensory issue

• define together which Pathway redirection tool would be best for her

• put him in charge of his own redirection, e.g., he chooses when it's time to take a break.

Clarify Protocols for Meeting Components

Smooth arrival and message interactions

If students arrive all at once or in large groups and are therefore unable to read and respond to the daily news in a timely manner:

- Check the hallways to see if students are delaying coming into the room in order to socialize. Explain to them why they need to come into the room promptly. After they read and respond to the message, they can chat with others in the room and take a seat in the circle.

- If the mass arrival is unchangeable, you may need to limit the interactivity of your daily news messages and place the chart where the whole group can read it simultaneously.

Smooth transition to circle

If creating the circle takes too long and is cutting into meeting time:

- Consider having your last class of the afternoon take care of this. Of course, set expectations and practice the process with them.

- Ask students who arrive early to create the circle.

- Try again! After modeling and practicing, students should be able to quietly move furniture and create a circle in a minute or less. Think about whether you've thoroughly modeled and practiced with students how to do this, and/or have a buy-in conversation with them (see below, Endorsement/Coming to circle, page 63.

Set the right greeting pace

If a formal greeting (one at a time, around the circle), whip or dialogue share, or game is taking too long, and the reason why is unclear, set an expectation that includes a pacing element. Share with students how much time you have allotted for the greeting and how to be successful:

Our greeting should make it around the circle in two minutes. That means each individual greeting will have to be completed in six seconds, and that includes turning to face the next person. I'll time us. I may let you know how long each greeting is taking, so you can get a feel for how this should be paced. Remember, the audience's role is always to watch silently and honor the greeting as it moves around the room. Watching quietly will help keep the pace up.

Coach eye contact when greeting

Without eye contact, greetings lose some of their positive energy. Eye contact is often more difficult for the responder, who might turn away too soon. Model and practice keeping eye contact throughout the greeting. Cultural issues regarding eye contact may arise. For example, some students may have been taught to show respect by avoiding eye contact. Consult local experts to find out what the norms are.

When possible, check with family members before the school year begins or as soon as possible, so the community can respect diversity.

Model how to quickly return to watching and honoring the greeting until it has made its way around the circle. It's common for students to take too long to do this. Setting a clear "honor the greeting" rule and enforcing it helps eliminate side conversations.

Support interactive sharing

To master interactive sharing, both sharer and audience need support. The audience's role may be more important to the success of an interactive share than the role of the person sharing. Model and practice how to give a clear, concise opening share, how to listen, how to make a respectful, on-topic comment, and how to ask an open-ended question. The first few times you use this format, have the audience form partnerships and plan some questions ahead of time. Set time aside to check in with the student(s) who will share before they do so. Make sure their shares are relevant to the topic and appropriate to the advisory setting.

Open-ended questions elicit more (and more interesting) information from the sharer than simpler, yes-or-no ones do, and they keep the audience attentive with curiosity, empathy, and interest. Consider the following two questions after Kalvina shares, "I went to an all-you-can-eat-buffet with my aunt last night."

Tecla: "Was it fun?"

Kalvina: "Yes."

Gina: "What did you notice about the other guests in the restaurant?"

Kalvina: "There was a big group who were celebrating a kid's tenth birthday. They brought in their own cake and were singing and laughing as they talked about the birthday girl. At another table..."

An interactive share without open-ended questions runs the risk of leading nowhere, and in their boredom, the audience can become inattentive. Questions like Gina's are much more interesting.

Create a chart that includes open-ended question starters, and post it near your meeting space. Announce an expectation that audience members will use one of the examples from the list or create an open-ended question of their own. Example question starters:

- Describe...
- Compare....
- Tell more about...
- What was your favorite part, and why?
- Please explain....

Balance share participation

Extroverts usually want to share a lot and to ask lots of questions, and introverts usually are the opposite. Building a strong learning community requires the active, fairly balanced participation of all. Whip shares and partner shares help equalize participation, and should be used at the beginning of the year to create a culture of participation.

When the group is ready for interactive sharing, create a calendar that indicates when one or two students will lead an interactive share. Make sure everyone has had a chance to lead one share before anyone leads a second one.

Manage the audience's role to ensure as much balance as possible:

- Limit everyone to one question per share.

- Pull sticks or in another way randomize who asks a question.

- Establish an expectation of no stealing the spotlight: never allow someone to take over someone else's share.

Raise expectations to match higher-level activities

If you've tried one or two higher-risk activities (games involving contact, movement, drama, content-area knowledge, etc.) and students were not successful, you might need to be extra careful about setting expectations when you move to higher-level activities. Be transparent as you model and practice the new game:

Today we're going to try something new, and it has a couple of risky parts. Watch and think carefully. We haven't tried anything this complex yet, so let's see how we do.

Watch carefully, and assess: perhaps you jumped too quickly to a higher-risk game, or perhaps the jump was too far (from low-risk to high-risk, skipping medium-risk). Return to the level where the group was successful, and resume climbing toward more challenge again, only a bit more slowly. See above, Teacher Preparation/Plan appropriate content, page 43, for more information.

Set up argument-free activities

If activities are getting bogged down in arguments over issues of fair play, take time to discuss and practice the art of winning and losing gracefully. This skill builds resilience.

- Invoke a "tagger's choice" rule or equivalent: the tagger decides whether she tagged you or not.

- Use rock-paper-scissors to settle disputes. Discuss the advantages of using a system like this.

- Stop the game. Perhaps you should use temporary Loss of Privilege or Fix It on the Spot. Review expectations; speak about the importance of following the expectations, then resume the game. If the group still fails to follow expectations, stop the game and spend the next few days playing lower-level games. Then try again: reset the expectations, recall what happened last time, have the group predict the consequences of successful play this time, and start again. Sooner or later, they are bound to get it! See Chapter Seven: Pathways to Self-control for reflection on and strategies for improving redirection.

Resource: See *Classroom Discipline*, pages 162-169, for more about Loss of Privilege and Fix It on the Spot.

Use the Loop to teach problem-solving

Young people love to play, but they aren't always good at playing cooperatively and positively. They quarrel, they get confused, and at times they break the rules. But because they want to continue to play, they are interested in reflecting on how things went and on fixing what went wrong. Use the Loop to review the game and improve it for next time. For example, during the game, stop the action to ask: What do you notice about the way we're playing? At the end of the game, ask: What was fun about the game? Consider whether the game was safe and fair. Are any improvements necessary? Are there any problems to solve? Then plan for next time: What can we add to the game to make it more energetic (or safer, or more inclusive, etc.)?

By identifying problems and finding solutions, students experience taking responsibility for the success of the activities, and feelings of both competence and autonomy grow.

ACCOUNTABILITY

Once expectations have been modeled and practiced, nothing other than following the protocol is acceptable. You have the job of holding students accountable—a vital role to maintain the firm ground on which the group builds a safe community. Abundant suggestions follow, but see also below, Chapter Seven: Pathways to Self-control for reflection on and strategies for improving redirection.

Model, then practice, then enforce

Modeling and practicing any routine happens *no more than* three times. Consistent enforcement is the hardest part, and it happens all day, every day. It can be exhausting early in the year, but done right, it leads to a year of lively, respectful, successful learning.

Resource: See *Classroom Discipline*, Chapters Seven and Eight, for Pathways redirection and problem-solving tools that get students quickly and effectively back on track.

Mindsets are key

Action and objective mindsets are particularly important when holding students accountable. Teachers need to embrace their job of maintaining the integrity of the rules without taking offense when students deviate from expectations. Each time we redirect a student to the rules, we show belief in their capacity to grow and do better. See Chapter Two: Mindsets Create the Tone of Teaching for characteristics of teacher mindsets and how to maintain them.

Review your endorsement

A *Developmental Designs* slogan for accountability is "sweat the small stuff." The danger of letting small things slide, or choosing your battles, is escalation to larger problems. Failure to "sweat it" can give students the impression that you do not take the rules seriously.

Bedrock of a safe community

Accountability matters at all times, but the goal of community building in advisory raises the stakes for those twenty minutes. By practicing equitable and compassionate behavior management while guarding the group's rules, you model how to treat others all the time.

The first six weeks

After you establish an expectation, consistently redirect whenever any student does not follow the model or in any way breaks the Social Contract. For example, as soon as someone mumbles a name in a greeting, stop the greeting, calmly ask for a redo, then move on. The first few weeks, when students closely observe whether you mean what you say about the rules, are crucial.

Develop and maintain consistency

Plan ahead how you will consistently hold students accountable to your expectations. For example, a few language prompts, such as *Let's back up and try this again, only this time, let's follow the rules* and similar phrases, can help you respond equitably and calmly to rule breaking.

Build trust by holding everyone accountable

Even students who rarely break rules need redirection when they do. When you hold everyone equally accountable for the rules, students trust that your redirections are fair. Make a point of using as many of the Pathways tools as possible with as many students as possible so they see that Pathways is for everyone.

- Direct a respected leader, like the student council president, to take a break (TAB) and then, in the same meeting, a frequent disruptor. Students will see that TAB is for everyone.

- When a student blurts out, use Fix It on the Spot: intervene, restart the greeting, or back it up a step or two, and this time, make sure the student waits his turn. Later, when someone else blurts, use a nonverbal cue, TAB, or redirecting language. Then debrief, so students see that fair doesn't mean exactly the same thing for everyone: different tools work for different people.

- If a student balks at a redirect, conference with her as soon as possible, and come up with a tool that she thinks has the best chance of working for her— give her a say.

Your message is: *When you break a rule, I will redirect you. It would not be fair for me to let one student get by with something and redirect another. But how I redirect each student is up to me. Sometimes I'll use one tool for one student and a different tool for another student who broke the same rule. This is how Pathways works. It's fair for everyone, but not the same for everyone.*

Keep your redirections prompt and equitable. Students will appreciate it.

Make room for, and minimize, delays

Quick and equitable redirection allows meetings to keep moving at an engaging pace. Frustrating though it is at times, accountability is more important than timing and flow in advisory meetings. Stopping to redirect or remind students may throw off your meeting's pace, but it facilitates fluid meetings in the long run.

Allow time for interruptions when you are establishing advisory in the first six weeks of school, and when you introduce a new challenge, or students return after a break, and at other times that might require more redirection and reminders. Keep at least one component brief and simple, and you'll be able to conduct a complete meeting within the timeframe, while holding everyone accountable.

Involve students in tracking success

Accentuate the positive by having students track their successful behaviors during greeting or sharing. For example, have them tally the number of greetings that fulfill expectations. Then ask: *How many successful greetings did we have today?* The group can set goals and celebrate with a favorite game when they reach them.

Invite students to hold you accountable

Ask students to help you improve a teaching skill. For example, if you want to work on greeting students at the door before the bell rings, have them tally the number of days each week that you do so. Ask them for a few seconds of feedback after the bell rings. They will see that accountability applies to you, too.

Accountability Fosters Relationship

When you redirect students fairly and respectfully, your relationships with everyone in the class are strengthened. Students see that you believe in their capacity for goodness and are committed to helping them. The message is: *We all make mistakes. My job is to help you get back on track so you can be successful.*

Resources: For ways to introduce students to redirections that build relationship and maximize endorsement, see *Developmental Designs 1 Resource Book*, pages 150-152, and *Developmental Designs 2 Resource Book*, pages 126-127.

Choose the Right Redirection

Pathways is a differentiated system of behavior management that helps us respond to misbehavior according to students' needs and developmental levels. Use your knowledge of students, including creating or reviewing Student Profiles, to differentiate your responses. For example:

- A student seeking ways to avoid work should probably not be told to take a break. Choose a redirect that has a better chance of keeping him engaged, like changing his seat, or redirecting language.

- If a student's rule breaking seems related to a need to pause to refresh her focus, take a break would be a useful redirection.

- A power-struggler or attention-seeker should not receive added power or attention when you redirect her. Instead, use Fix It on the Spot or a nonverbal cue or a quick conference. These tools include less opportunity for arguing or negotiating.

- A student who needs to move away from a stimulus in order to calm down should not receive a redirect that makes her stay in her current location; instead, she should be told to take a break or to change her seat (Loss of Privilege).

- A student who thinks literally and concretely may not be able to read a subtle cue like quietly saying his name or telling him to take a break. Instead, use redirecting language or a quick conference.

Hold yourself accountable

If you break a rule, redirect yourself. Briefly explain what you are doing, then go to TAB or use Fix It on the Spot. Students will see your integrity and know you are with them all the way.

Quick conference to find the right redirection

When you are not immediately sure how to respond, a quick conference with a student might reveal a response that the student will endorse. Later, holding him accountable will be easier because you have partnered with him for his success. Some students may need to hear multiple versions of this message as you hold them accountable: *I'll never give up on you, and I'm always going to hold you accountable to the rules. Let's keep working at this until we find a path that leads to growth.*

Support struggling students strategically

If most students greet, share, and play according to the rules, but a few struggle, try these supports:

- Seat struggling students strategically; don't allow them to make poor seating decisions.

- Quick-conference regularly and individually with struggling students. The goal of each conference is to check in on what's working, what isn't, and what strategies the two of you can use in the immediate future.

- In most cases, struggling students should have a fresh start each morning, but Loss of Privilege (separation from the meeting, or from one or more of its components) for two or three days works well for some.

- Of course, it depends. If the struggler wants to avoid participation, choose a path that keeps him in the meeting and as participatory as possible. If nothing seems to help, seek support from colleagues to find a response that moves the student forward.

See above, Expectations/When clear expectations aren't enough, page 49, for more ways to support struggling students.

Bring Rigor to All Participation

Require appropriate sharing content and conduct

If students select inappropriate topics and/or speak too casually as they share or ask questions, it may be related to insufficiently clear expectations or insufficient teacher preparation. If you have provided a list of appropriate topics and set clear expectations for self-selected topics (e.g. they must be school-appropriate and respect the privacy and dignity of every group member) and have established expectations for voice levels and content, accountability may be the issue. Try:

- If a student shares something or asks a question that may cause trouble or embarrassment for another, cut her off immediately: *Danielle, we do not share that type of thing in our meetings.* Tell her to switch to a school-appropriate topic or to share at a later date.

  You may wish to help her save face: *Danielle. I should have checked in with you before you began, to make sure what you had in mind was appropriate. I'm sorry I didn't, and I'll make sure to do that in the future.* If you think she meant to share inappropriate information to get attention, help her choose an appropriate topic for next time that will fulfill that need in a pro-social way.

- If you notice that students receive negative attention during sharing, address the issue generally the following day or soon thereafter. Accept the need for attention but not that way of fulfilling the need:

  Everyone needs attention. A sharer gets a moment in the spotlight, and each of us gets attention when we ask a question of the sharer. The attention has to be positive. It has to follow our Social Contract, and it has to respect everyone's privacy. I will do better at holding everyone accountable to these expectations, and you all need to keep your questions and responses appropriate.

Require interaction with the daily news

If students skip reading and responding to the message, try these accountability approaches:

- Give a friendly reminder as you greet each student as they arrive.
- Assign each student a number, and have each one write their number beside their response on the chart. Keep track of the students who have not responded, and huddle up with them to problem-solve.

Require appropriate responses to the daily news

If students respond inappropriately, announce the problem: *Some of us are writing incomplete or inappropriate comments on the daily news chart. This has to stop.* Some possible solutions:

- Assign students a number to use on the interactive portion of the message and hold them accountable for responding beside that number until further notice.

- Require everyone to add their name or initials to their comments. This way, you can keep track of the number of appropriate, successful interactions and redirect or conference with those who are off-track.

- For several days, greet everyone at the door and remind them to respond appropriately.

ENDORSEMENT

Just as we share the rationale for learning in content areas with students, we need to explain to them why CPR and A+ meetings are worth their time. Advisory experiences teach explicit skills, relevant to both the social and academic realms. Grades are not given, nor learning targets usually identified, and growth in skills may not be apparent, but these advisory meetings teach and provide practice in information and skills essential to success in life. Students are more likely to endorse advisory meetings if they see the relevance to their lives.

Advisory groups meet for three important purposes:

1. To cultivate the conditions for learning in community, especially when students from various cultures coexist but may not understand or appreciate each other

2. To teach and practice social-emotional, intellectual, and organizational skills for success

3. To address student needs pro-socially, including needs for relationship, fun, competence, and autonomy.

Consider sharing these, or have a group conversation to articulate and endorse the meetings' purposes. If students take some ownership of the meetings, they will participate more.

Mind your Mindsets

Creating student endorsement relies on teacher endorsement for energy and inspiration. To have and to share positive energy, teachers need constructive mindsets for the daily challenges of teaching. Before beginning an endorsing conversation with students, reflect on your own disposition toward the meetings, including your mindsets. Resolve that students will take on the goal of interesting, fun, growth-filled advisory meetings and you will guide them every step of the way. See the Strategies for Nurturing Your Growth Mindset section in Chapter Two, page 20.

Project a positive attitude

Students watch you closely, including your tone and body language. Share your positive attitude about advisory.

Participate consistently

Engage in the meetings enthusiastically: greet and share authentically and according to the protocol; be playful, interested, and invested. Never abandon your role as the professional leader: when students miss the mark, guide them back.

Relationship and mindset combine to build endorsement

As you participate in the meetings and manage student behavior, you model and grow in relationship. Your mindset colors your words, actions, and body language and creates the quality of your relationships. As you model respectful, friendly, full participation, students are more likely to buy into and participate in the meetings.

Finding Time for Endorsing Conversations

You may ask: When is there time to have these conversations? Advisory is brief, and the format leaves little time for additions.

Many opportunities for student buy-in are built into *Developmental Designs* practices. The modeling format seeks and invites student endorsement at every step, as do the Loop, written reminders, and Pathways. All the students in the school helped create and explicitly endorsed the Social Contract (admittedly, some more reluctantly than others). CPR meetings have implicit student endorsement built in: responding to the message, greeting, sharing, and playing together all take a certain level of endorsement.

You can increase explicit endorsement at various times, whenever you feel it's necessary, during meetings.

Increase endorsement at the beginning

Have a quick conversation with the group about the value of a new greeting, share, or activity as you model it. Explain its relevance and examine its skills and payoffs: *What skills will help you in this game? What are the payoffs of playing this game as co-operatively as possible?* If the game is competitive: *What are the payoffs of staying in a game as long as you can, and gracefully bowing out if you are eliminated?* There is more below about using modeling for endorsement.

Increase endorsement along the way

When you plan to use a familiar greeting, sharing format, or activity, before beginning it, quickly share a connection, story, metaphor, diagram, or other brief way to increase or maintain student endorsement. Before and after the experience, the Loop can call attention to payoffs: *What social skill(s) did you use as you played this game?* There is more below about using the Loop for endorsement.

These quick diversions take no more than a minute, and they are well worth the time to increase student understanding and buy-in.

Use Activity Plus for intentional endorsement

The extended activity time and reflection built into the A+ meetings are well suited for delving deeper into discussions about endorsement. Consider these possibilities:

- Do a read-aloud with text focused on a real-life benefit of strong community. See *The Advisory Book*, page 105, for the read-aloud activity structure.

- Do a Stop-and-Think Modeling about managing competition in activities. Extend the conversation during the reflection to how these skills might come in handy outside of school. See *The Advisory Book*, page 115.

- Add character and specialness to your advisory space. See *The Advisory Book*, page 107.

- Use the pre-planned A+ advisory Social Skills Group Work to draw out skills. See *The Advisory Book*, page 161.

Browse the many pre-planned Activity Plus advisories in *The Advisory Book* for more boosting endorsement ideas.

Use modeling to build endorsement

Enlist the students in identifying why advisory or a certain component is important and worth the time it takes. The steps of modeling take care of some of this when students are asked questions like:

- Why is it important to take a little time each day to greet each other, even on days when we're in a hurry or not in the mood?

- What skills do you need when you're having a one-to-one conversation?

- What's in it for you if you greet someone with eye contact, an authentic smile, and correct name pronunciation?

- What's going to be challenging about playing this active game safely in a tight circle, and how can we overcome these challenges?

Use the Loop to Notice and Acknowledge

The Loop is inherently an endorsement-boosting tool because it includes student input in each of its three phases. The more students realize that you care about their ideas enough to include their voices in the decision-making process about how a greeting, share, or activity should go, the more they will buy in.

Loop to notice skills

Help students see benefits as their skills develop. As CPR work progresses, help them reflect on gains they have made in trust, relationship, and social skills. Continue to invite them to appreciate their value and to embrace the rationale for this work. Engage students with the Loop during each component of the meeting, frequently inviting them to anticipate targeted social skills and relationship-building and reflecting after activities about results and next steps. Point out which skills are being practiced, and make connections between these skills and life outside of school.

Resource: Empower students to reflect and assess the meetings themselves. See the article *Coaches' Corner: Score Your Advisories*, by Scott Tyink, at www.DevelopmentalDesigns.org

Loop to notice needs addressed

When students see that teachers plan and reflect on how to address their needs, they take note: *S/he sees parts of who I am and tries to make advisory work for me.* You can invite students into the Loop by asking need-related questions such as:

- **Need for fun:** *How could we adjust this game so it's even sillier?*

- **Need for autonomy and competence:** *Reflect on your greeting skills. Who thinks they might be ready to choose or lead the greeting for one of our meetings next week?*

- **Need for relationship:** *What is one question we could have asked Sarah during sharing to learn more about her experience?*

Use Stories and Reflection to Build Endorsement

Guide students to see payoffs of skills learned in advisory with personal stories and student reflection on past experiences.

Personal story: Tell a story about how social skills or community groups have been important to you. Tell a story about how you have developed leadership skills and how these skills have helped you:

When I played _____, the team huddled frequently to discuss what was working, what wasn't, and to hear from the coach what to try next. Our advisory is like a huddle...

Connection to students' lives: Ask students how social skills such as respect, empathy, self-control, and cooperation have helped them in the past. Help them imagine how those skills will help them in the future:

How has being cooperative helped you in your family?

When has using self-control paid off for you? When has it saved you from trouble?

What jobs require people to manage conflict?

Talk with Individuals as Needed

While many quick endorsing conversations are accomplished during the meeting, with the whole group, they can also be very effective when an individual student needs extra support. When you have a hunch that a student's lack of robust participation reflects low buy-in, have a quick conference and draw out meaningful connections for them using stories and reflection questions as described above. Shape your inquiry for them individually: *I've noticed that you are good at sharing your soccer experiences. This is partly because of your interesting stories, and partly because of good questions from the audience. What could you gain from listening better when others are sharing or from learning how to ask open-ended questions?*

Defuse saboteurs

Sometimes a student seeks to sabotage what you are trying to accomplish. Have a quick conference with a saboteur as soon as you notice this. Saboteurs may need power, relationships, fun, or any combination of these. Try to learn in the conference what needs are motivating her/his behavior, then look for ways for her to meet those needs within the rules of the meeting.

Juan, the seventh grade committee in charge of selecting the theme for the spring play needs a couple of students to help them decide, and they need folks who can keep the decision a secret.

Jeanne, there's a game we could play in our meeting Friday that makes it appear that someone in our group has ESP and can use it to exchange information with someone else in the group. Are you interested in learning the role of the student with ESP? In exchange, you'll have to stop hassling what we're trying to accomplish during the meetings.

Resources:

- For quick conferencing, see *Classroom Discipline*, pages 50-55
- To address needs pro-socially, see *Classroom Discipline*, pages 277-280

Introduce One Component at a Time

Each component of CPR and A+ presents challenges that can raise student resistance. Greeting, sharing, activities, and reflecting include skills to be learned and reasons to work hard to master those skills.

Friendly but firm, especially in the first six weeks

As you establish advisory with a new group, there is a lot to learn and reinforce. During greetings, pauses occur for students to correct what they say or how they say it; many activities have to be interrupted for clarifications. Each time, your light, pleasant attitude will help keep endorsement high. The spirit to create is "we are all learning; mistakes are part of the process." The group could choose a phrase such as "roll back" or "do over" to signal that instant redo is necessary. Everyone will know what it means, and it will be an "in" term; when you use it, whoever needs to redo does so, and the meeting continues with a minimum of delay or embarrassment. You may need to add clarification following the phrase, but the process will be streamlined.

Coming to circle

I take time at the beginning of the school year, starting with my signal for attention and the circle formation, to explain why with students. I have found that if students get the rationale for meeting in a circle, they are on the path to appreciating the rationale for the rest of the CPR meeting components.

—Middle level educator

Connection to history

Talk with students about the history of meeting in a circle. Ask about student experiences with circle meetings (e.g., sports huddles, campfires, some religious practices, etc.) and its potential for strengthening the community in your advisory. Point out that no one in a circle is above or below anyone else. No one is inside or outside, and all are visible and equally vulnerable.

"Circles represent important principles in the Aboriginal worldview and belief systems, namely, interconnectedness, equality, and continuity. According to traditional teaching, the seasonal pattern of life and renewal and the movement of animals and people were continuous, like a circle, which has no beginning and no end. Circles suggest inclusiveness and lack of a hierarchy. They are found throughout nature – for instance, in the movement of the seasons and the sun's movement from east to west during the day. Circles are also used in the construction of teepees and sweat lodges; and the circular willow hoop, medicine wheel, and dream catcher are powerful symbols."[1]

Invite students to reflect on various formats used to conduct group business (e.g. classrooms with rows or tables, a stage or dais, an amphitheater) and help them see how structures can give messages or support goals. Challenge them to look for other areas of their lives or society where circles are or could be useful.

Resource: For a broad view of the power of the circle, see *An Excellent Medium: Equity in a Circle*, by Todd Bartholomay, at www.DevelopmentalDesigns.org.

Signal for attention

Because the signal is very important and is used frequently, student endorsement is critical. Everyone needs to agree to cooperate in its use.

Endorsing language: *Sometimes we need to settle down quickly and tune in. My signal will look like this and sound like this.*

See Strategies for Pathways to Self-control/Endorsement, below on page 132, for more details about building endorsement for the signal.

Greeting

Sample endorsing language: *Something positive we can do for each other every day is greet each other in a sincere way. We connect with each other and strengthen our community.*

Set an "honor the greeting" expectation. It helps students see that greetings are important, something to look forward to, and worth getting good at.

Endorsing language: *One routine way we'll greet each other will be to send "Good morning, _____" around the circle, one person at a time, until we've all been greeted. What should the rest of us be doing while we wait our turn and after we've had our turn? I want us to create and support a rule called "honor the greeting," which means silently watching each greeting, from the first to the last, and speaking only when it's our turn. In this way we will honor the importance of the friendly connections happening all the way around the circle. Let's try it.*

Explain the value of eye contact

Although eye contact isn't part of greeting in all communities, it is part of how we show connectedness in CPR and A+. Respectful eye contact can become an important skill beyond school.

Endorsing language: *In American society, eye contact is often an important part of greeting someone and showing that you are paying attention. It's not staring, which is disrespectful, and it's not glaring, which communicates anger or displeasure, and it is not the only custom. In our meetings, we will use friendly eye contact to communicate connection and caring.*

Sharing

Sharing is aimed at deepening relationships; developing lifelong listening and speaking skills; and exercising choice.

Resource: Read how one teacher invested students in CPR and school in general through a guided sharing process: *Add Some Quality to Your Sharing*, by Richard Frost, at www.DevelopmentalDesigns.org.

Endorsing language: *During sharing, we practice the art of conversation. Successful people connect through conversation. I want you to excel at this. You don't have to be a great public speaker—small talk is important, too. When people date, they chat as a way of getting to know each other. Business deals are conversations. International negotiations are conversations. Doctors and their patients converse. Teachers and students converse, and teachers and principals, and teachers and parents...you get the idea! That's how important our topic share this morning is.*

Activities

Saying some persuasive things about how the power of play can help students overcome hesitation they may have to participate fully.

Endorsing language: *Each morning, we will have a little fun together. We will play a wide variety of games. If you have positive, supportive fun together in the morning, you will be happier throughout the day, and you will actually learn more.*

Endorsing language: *Do you know the best way to learn something? To learn it while playing. When I was a kid running through our neighborhood with friends, I learned how to strategize, how to think on my feet, how to be as quiet as the night or as loud as a thunderstorm, how to force myself to hang in there when I was exhausted, how to make rules and handle disagreements, how to talk my mom into letting me stay outside longer. I hope you learn valuable things as we play games during our CPR. As we play, let's think sometimes about the skills we're working on—even if it doesn't feel like work!*

Endorsing language to address the group's comfort zones: *We'll try to choose games that are not too easy and not too hard. For starters, we'll play a few games I know we can be successful with, so we get comfortable and learn to create and follow rules together. This will help us keep things running smoothly when we get to more challenging games. My goal is for us to play much more challenging, higher-risk games as soon as we show that we are ready for them.*

Endorsing language to address individuals' comfort zones: *Each of us is different in what we're comfortable with and what we're more cautious about. We'll play thinking games, movement games, tag games, team games, games when we're all playing for ourselves, you name it. It will be very unusual if we play a game that 100 percent of us like or dislike. I challenge you to hang in there on days we play a game that you don't think you'll like, or a game you haven't enjoyed in the past. Sometimes if you give something outside your comfort zone a chance, you get a pleasant surprise.*

Play, which most students crave, requires enough safety for them to lower their defenses.

Endorsing language to support the Social Contract: *I watched a basketball game on TV this weekend. The home fans treated the visiting players terribly! They chanted insults and sang songs that mocked the other team's mistakes, and instead of being gracious winners, they were self-centered and childish. This kind of behavior is not a positive contribution to life.*

But in our classroom, we are going to restore civility in our games. Our Social Contract will guide our behavior, especially when we play something competitive, like our game today, Count to Ten. All of us will lose except one. Let's come up with a few ways we could quickly and respectfully express disappointment when we lose, and some empathy for the person who has to sit down, so we can move on with the fun and avoid the negativity I saw on TV. If we get good at winning and losing without leaving our dignity in tatters, we will develop resilience for life, when we lose things that are more important than a silly-but-fun game. Here's how to play.

Daily news

The daily news is an interactive vehicle for focusing student attention on priorities for the day. Much of the student endorsement of reading and responding to the daily news depends on the enjoyment and/or satisfaction they get reading it. Be sure the tone of the message is positive, the content relevant and respectful, and build fun into the message. It could be a word of the day, a riddle or joke, or an interactive question.

Appealing to students' need for autonomy can also encourage them to endorse the advisory process: *The daily news helps you be independent. Before I wrote daily news messages, students had to ask me, "What are we doing today?" Now, all you have to do is read the message.*

Student-led CPR

Students must be socially ready to lead CPR. Share with students your vision of student-led meetings.

Endorsing language: *Starting next week, I'm going to begin to hand over to you, bit by bit, the responsibility of leading our CPR meetings. You've earned it.*

Endorsing language: *CPR time can also be leadership-training time. We have __ meetings left this year, and I want each of you to lead one. You are future leaders, and there's no time like the present to start leading.*

Vary Content to Maintain Endorsement

When we prepare CPR meetings that match students' current levels of skill and community development, we build endorsement. Continually assess the readiness level of your group. As the school year progresses, sequence the greetings, shares, and activities so they grow more challenging. Otherwise, the group can get into a rut or lose focus, playing games that are too hard one day, too easy the next. Questions to ask yourself:

- Do I use the meetings to pro-socially meet students' need for autonomy, fun, relationship, and competence?

- Do I select greetings, shares, activities, and daily news messages that fit my group?

See above, Teacher Preparation/Plan appropriate contents, page 43, for more ideas and references.

Resource: *The Advisory Book*, Assessing Social Skills in CPR Tool, page 267

ENGAGEMENT

Engagement relies on relationship and endorsement. Read through the relevant sections above for more ideas. If enthusiasm for advisory seems low, consider these adjustments.

Meet Students' Needs

Autonomy: solicit and integrate student feedback

When their need for having a say is met, students are happier.

- Use the Loop to include students in the daily process of planning and reflecting. When possible, integrate their ideas and interests into the meetings.

- Together, keep a list of games you've played. Add games to the list as they are introduced. Over time, group favorites will emerge. Allow students to choose the game sometimes. The same could be done with greetings and sharing formats and topics.

- Ask students how the meetings could be more fun. Write down their suggestions and implement some of them for a week or two, then assess them with the group, and make adjustments as necessary.

Resource: Read how one teacher reinvigorated her advisory group by asking, "What are we going to do to take care of our community?" See article *The Power of Ownership*, by Ann Larson Ericson, at www.DevelopmentalDesigns.org.

Competence and fun: match the challenge to the group's skills

- When the group is ready, move gradually to student-led CPRs. Look for signs of consistent self-control and enthusiastic participation before turning control over to students. See *The Advisory Book*, pages 89-97, for a step-by-step description of implementing student-led CPRs.

- Continually assess the group's skills and trust level, and plan meetings that provide moderate challenge. Under- or over-challenging can shut down engagement. Choose content for each component so that as social skills and positive community grow, the group gradually experiences more challenge. See above, Teacher Preparation/Plan appropriate content, page 43.

Relationship: tend to community safety

- Students might not feel safe in the circle. When this happens, you will notice their anxiety; their body language and manner of speaking (e.g., slouching, mumbling, hesitation) will be a tip-off. You may need to back up and use lower-risk components. Play collaborative team-building and trust-building games when students are ready.

  Reflect on the degree to which you have modeled, practiced, and enforced basic pro-social behaviors like listening, responding quickly to the signal for attention, raising hands and waiting to be called on before speaking, winning and losing gracefully, and behaving according to the Social Contract. Stating expectations and holding students accountable to them builds and strengthens community. See more ideas above in Expectations and Accountability.

- Watch for bullying and/or sabotage, and intervene quickly by conferencing individually with perpetrators. Straight talk is the key: name the problem, state why the bullying or sabotage must stop, and together plan a strategy for stopping it immediately. See *Classroom Discipline*, page 194, for quick and full conference instruction.

Resource: Read how one teacher created safe, full CPR participation for all students in the article *Engagement for All*, by Melanie Kirner, at www.DevelopmentalDesigns. org.

Bring Rigor and Relevance to the Daily News

When students seem disengaged with the daily news message, reinforce the routine:

- Include information that is engaging and relevant. Include interactive questions or prompts. Try a daily fun fact, riddle, or joke. Include news about the progress the group is making on a project. When they're ready, hand over to them the responsibility for writing parts of or the whole message.

- Be sure you have made clear your expectations for reading and responding to the message, then consistently hold them accountable. Some possible supports:

  For several days, greet everyone at the door and remind them to respond.

  Require them to add their name or initials to their comments.

  Assign each student a number. Have them respond in writing to the message, placing their number by their response. This provides both accountability and anonymity.

- Make sure to return to the message at the end of the meeting for a group reading.

- Perhaps model or remodel for the exact routine for arriving and reading the message.

CHAPTER FOUR

Goal Setting and the Social Contract

REFLECTING ON GOAL SETTING AND THE SOCIAL CONTRACT

Activate your *growth mindset* as you consider this vision for goal setting and collaborative rule making. Reflect on the degree to which you engage best practices. Even in the strongest practice, there is always room for growth. Even in a beginning practice, there is always evidence of strength. Take stock, then select what you want to work on.

Goal Setting

1. **Creating the conditions:** Do I explain why setting personal goals is important?

2. **Creating the conditions:** Do I inspire students to aim high by sharing stories of people who set and achieve(d) their goals?

3. **Creating the conditions:** Do I provide good examples of student-generated goals?

4. **Form:** Do I require actionable goals to be written in the form of declarations ("I will...") and provide examples for support?

5. **Recording/Display:** Do I provide examples to help students develop creative and visually appealing displays of their written goals?

6. **Follow-up:** Do I check in on goals throughout the year to keep students connected to and revising their personal social and academic goals?

Social Contract

1. **Development:** Do students and I create and come to consensus on three to five brief, broad classroom rules? Are they posted in the room for easy reference?

2. **Goals connection:** Do students have opportunities to reflect on their goals and declarations and connect them to the process of creating rules?

3. **Positively stated:** Is our Social Contract stated as a set of ideal behaviors: what to do (e.g., stay positive, respect others), rather than negatives?

4. **Application:** Do I refer to the Social Contract throughout the school year and in different contexts to assess behavior, reinforce positive behavior, and redirect rule breaking?

5. **Application:** As necessary, do I reconnect students to the purpose of the Social Contract as a guide to behavior and academic performance?

BARRIERS TO GOAL SETTING AND THE SOCIAL CONTRACT

Identify barriers

What gets in the way of effective goal-setting and an effective Social Contract? Review what other teachers identify as barriers to growth in advisory. Keeping in mind the goal-setting or Social Contract element you've selected to work on, identify the common barriers to growth that fit your experience.

Identify strategy areas

The barriers are grouped into the six strategy areas: Relationship, Teacher Preparation, Expectations, Accountability, Endorsement, and Engagement. Identify the strategy area most relevant to your experience. For example, if barriers described under Endorsement reflect some of what you observe in students or yourself, start by reading that Strategies section on page 82.

Common Barriers to Growth

Relationship

Students do not work well together or cannot reach agreement for the Contract.

Students do not seem willing to share their personal interests.

Teacher Preparation

There isn't enough time for students to set goals, follow up on goals throughout the year, and/or create a Social Contract.

I am unclear about or forgot the steps of the goal-setting process or creating a Social Contract.

I need more ideas for the goal-setting and/or Social Contract process, including storytelling and inspiration for displays.

My school's common rules are already set and can't be changed.

Expectations

I do not require students to set meaningful personal goals.

Students come up with too many rules and/or want to use negative ("Don't") language.

Students sabotage the creation of a Contract.

Accountability

I need more ideas for and structures to support ways to check in on goals meaningfully.

We create a Social Contract, but we rarely refer to it once it is up on the wall.

I refer to the Social Contract mostly when rules are broken and rarely to reinforce positive behavior.

Students want to but do not yet have some of the skills necessary to abide by the Contract.

Endorsement

I am uncertain about the value of the goal-setting and Contract creation process:

- their introduction through examples and storytelling
- their power in guiding behavior or growth
- the necessity of follow-up— keeping the rules alive and pursuing personal goals past the start of the year

Students do not see the importance of setting goals.

Students do not see the benefits of participating in rule creation.

Engagement

Students are not interested in setting personal goals. They see it as extra work.

Students show little interest in creating a Social Contract and offer few ideas.

I use other redirection and reinforcement tools and rarely use the Social Contract to guide behavior.

STRATEGIES FOR GOAL SETTING AND THE SOCIAL CONTRACT

The strategies are organized into six areas: Relationship, Teacher Preparation, Expectations, Accountability, Endorsement, and Engagement. Follow these steps to make the most of the detailed suggestions provided:

1. Read Chapter Two: Mindsets Create the Tone of Teaching as context for all the strategies.
2. Read the strategies areas identified by your review of Barriers to Goal Setting and the Social Contract.
3. Follow suggestions and your interest to read other, related areas.

General resources

Find specific resources referenced throughout the strategies, e.g., an article about creating endorsement. Explore the following *Developmental Designs* resources for additional, detailed support for goal setting and creating the Social Contract:

- *Developmental Designs 1 Resource Book*
- *Developmental Designs 2 Resource Book*
- *The Advisory Book: Building a Community of Learners Grades 5-9*
- *Classroom Discipline: Guiding Adolescents to Responsible Independence*
- www.DevelopmentalDesigns.org (free articles, meeting content, and other resources)
- http://www.YouTube.com/user/DevelopmentalDesigns (see practices in action)

RELATIONSHIP

At the beginning of the year, when everyone is getting to know each other, use the goal-setting process to learn about students' aspirations. Use it to prompt students to reflect on their connections to learning, and to share insights and stories about having goals in school and in other areas of life; this creates a rich context for setting goals for the year and for choosing three or four fundamental rules that will help the class toward their goals.

It takes time to develop a safe community in which students can express their interests and goals. They may not be willing to share their personal goals right away. *The Advisory Book* includes a sequence of advisory meeting formats ideal for the first few weeks of school. This group of advisories is oriented toward getting acquainted, declaring individual goals for the year, then creating and endorsing a social contract of three to five basic rules to help everyone reach their goals. In the process, everyone creates an attractive expression of their goals, and all of these are composed into a display which will be near the contract when it is completed. See page 136 in *The Advisory Book.*

See strategies for increasing student investment under Endorsement and ideas for sparking the process under Teacher Preparation.

Consensus process builds relationship

Creating and endorsing the Social Contract strengthens connection among everyone in the classroom community. The process requires students to listen carefully to one another, disagree respectfully, and make compromises. See strategies in Expectations, below, for students who struggle with these skills.

Everyone participates

Participate in the process by setting your own goals for the year and sharing them with the students. Tell why you chose your goal(s), and include them in the artistic display. Participate in the creation of the Social Contract; help students understand what rules must be addressed to help everyone reach their goals. Respect and listen to every student; the more participation in creating the rules, the more endorsement and cooperation throughout the year.

TEACHER PREPARATION

Efficient, well-prepared guidance of goal setting and Social Contract development is a strong beginning for the mutual respect you want all year. In the goal-setting and Contract-creating process, you show that you respect students' aspirations and voices, and they experience your respectful authority. Review the steps of each process on pages 55-59 in the *Developmental Designs 1 Resource Book*.

Find time for class and school-wide rules

Once advisory or homeroom Social Contracts have been established, team and/or school-wide expectations can flow from them. The advisory or homeroom may elect delegates to a special "convention" to create the team or school-wide contract, or the student council or social studies teacher(s) may lead a contract-creating process. The school could conclude the process on Constitution Day, September 17, to add historic perspective to their democratic process.

Resource: The Constitutional Convention process is described in detail in *Classroom Discipline*, pages 76-77, and in *Developmental Designs 1 Resource Book*, pages 66-67.

If your scope is limited to your students in content classes or your advisory, consider using time set aside for orientation and establishing behavior expectations to set goal and create Contract rules. If you usually do some sort of community-building or introductions to your subject areas at the start of the year, then goal setting and Contract creation can serve these purposes nicely. In other words, if you can't find additional instruction time, review your start of the year work for ways to integrate these processes. See below under Accountability for ways to find time to follow through on goals and keep the Contract alive and effective.

A spark for goal-setting

Introduce the goal-setting process with a "spark" that creates an atmosphere of hope, inspiration, and striving. It can be a quote, a poem, a short story, a movie clip, etc. A story about what inspires you and what you aspire to helps students get to know you and might inspire them to share about their own hopes and what motivates them. Share how you got inspired, how this shapes your goals, what action you have taken, and how things are going. These details will provide a map for the goal-setting process: how do I seek inspiration, generate goals, and take action?

Resources:
Classroom Discipline, pages 256-257
Developmental Designs 1 Resource Book, pages 56-58

Plan for displaying goals

Displaying everyone's goals strengthens the classroom community and provides a visual reminder of how we expressed the value of school and why it is important that we work hard and maintain self-control. An image like a quilt or a building reinforces the principle that we are all in this together. Templates for recording goals are available in *Developmental Designs 1 Resource Book*, pages 60-62.

The inspiration you choose to launch the process can influence the display. For example, if you use the story of The Coyote and the Whippoorwill (*Developmental Designs 1 Resource Book*, pages 57-58) as the spark, students might write their declarations inside a whippoorwill shape, decorated and displayed together as a flock. If many of your students want to keep their goals private, post the declarations in sealed, decorated envelopes. One teacher had students put their goals in envelopes, then bundled them together and hung them from the ceiling with colorful yarn to remind them of their lofty goals.

Display the Social Contract

As you arrange your classroom at the start of the year, reserve some prime wall space for the Social Contract. It should be easy to see and read from anywhere in the room. Considering that students might move about and sit facing in different directions at different times, you might want to display copies of the Contract on more than one wall, visually emphasizing that the Contract, formulated and endorsed by all, is the foundation for all the behavior expectations that you will enforce throughout the year.

Congruity with school rules

If your school implements *Developmental Designs* practices school-wide, creating an all-school Social Contract through a process like the Constitutional Convention establishes common expectations throughout the building and includes student endorsement. Then every teacher makes clear to students how living up to the expectations will look in his or her classroom and in communal spaces like lavatories, hallways, and the lunchroom. Through modeling, practicing, and visual reminders, students can learn or recall what respect looks, sounds, and feels like when we are moving through the cafeteria line; what "responsibility" means in our science lab; and so on.

Even if you are one of only a few teachers who use *Developmental Designs* practices in your school, the consensus-generated Social Contract is a powerful way to set expectations in your classroom. It is likely that your classroom rules will resemble and reinforce the school rules. Once both sets of rules exist, you can help students make connections between them.

EXPECTATIONS

Routines that support order and productivity

Before you begin goal setting, teach a few basic routines to facilitate the process: the signal for attention, how to listen to each other, how to respond to a redirect, how to use writing utensils, how to come to consensus, and how to use any special tools or materials related to the creation of the attractive display of the goals.

Set challenging, reachable goals

Samples help students create meaningful, realistic goals. You can create a set of sample goals for reading, writing, math, a social-emotional skill, and perhaps a goal outside of school. Begin each goal with "I will...." Share these examples with students before they write their own, and explain why each one is a "quality goal"— something worth striving for.

To make sure goals are reachable, use SMART goals: Specific, Measurable, Attainable, Realistic, and Time-bound. Examples of SMART goals are: *I will read outside of school for at least 20 minutes Monday through Thursday for the next two weeks. I will complete and turn in on time all my homework assignments for the next two weeks.* These might be quality goals for one student but not for another; see below Accountability/Require student participation for a discussion of this issue.

Resource: Review the steps of creating an engaging goal-setting process in the article *Creating Declarations* by Christopher Hagedorn at www.DevelopmentalDesigns. org

A consensus process for rule-making

A "majority rules" structure leaves room for anyone to not endorse that rule and thereby claim immunity. Everyone needs to endorse the Contract. The reason for consensus-building is that everyone participates: everyone hears everyone. Thus aware of the diversity among their classmates, we hope that students become willing to compromise for the common good, finally reaching three or four simple, clear rules intended to guide all.

Students usually understand and engage in the give and take that's necessary for consensus, but occasionally someone holds out for his ideal, or simply to sabotage the process, causing it to stall. Any student who does not agree is expected to respectfully express their concern, and perhaps try to persuade others to their position. No one is allowed to refuse to consent without explanation.

If the process becomes emotional, you may need to take a break, and return to it the next day. Meanwhile, you can conference with the student(s) having difficulty with the process and craft a plan for the rest of the process. Do not retreat to a "majority rules" solution; this would undermine discipline for the rest of the year. Remind everyone that it may be that the minority have a good idea, and all should hear them out and consider their point of view.

Resource: See the consensus model in *Developmental Designs 1 Resource Book*, pages 66-67 and in *Classroom Discipline*, pages 74-76.

Guide positive Contract language

Explain to students that rules guide our behavior in a positive way. For example, if we state the rule, "Don't be mean," we have not created a guideline for what to do. Rules need to be stated positively, as guidelines for behavior. A positive guideline to replace "Don't be mean" could be "Treat people with respect." When someone phrases a rule negatively, ask, *If we need to not _____, then what should we do?*

Help students by laying out firm boundaries at the beginning of the process. Say that there will be no more than five rules, and each rule can have no more than three words. These boundaries require concision and careful thought about what words mean. The results will be easy to read and remember, with little wiggle room for misbehavior.

ACCOUNTABILITY

Require student participation

The power of the goal-setting process and the Social Contract is that they are founded in student participation. Have a conversation with any student who may have set an unrealistic or unchallenging goal for himself or herself. Begin by making sure you understand what they have written, and affirm that goal. Use your imagination to help the student use his or her imagination: *Deshawn, that's a great goal. Now let's connect it to school. How could this year in school help you achieve your goal of making the NBA?*

Sue, it will be fun for you to read all the Twilight books this year, but those books won't be challenging for you. In addition to that goal, I want you to set another goal that will stretch your reading skills. Let's think about that together.

Students' activities outside of school are important, too. You can gain insight into a student by learning about his passion and goals for skateboarding or hockey, and perhaps help him see that setting and pursuing academic goals is rewarding, too: *Ricardo, can you imagine setting a school goal and going after it until you achieve it? When you mess up on your board, what makes you get up and try again? Could you do that in our class?*

Some students might be reluctant to endorse the process and its outcomes, and therefore less likely to cooperate and succeed. Strategies for helping them are outlined below, in Endorsement.

Keeping goals alive

Help students keep their eyes on the prize. Reflect on their goals from time to time yourself, and refer to them in both planned and spontaneous conversations about a student's progress and wellbeing. Use reinforcing and reminding language to connect behavior to goals—when a goal seems unreachable to a student, you are the one who keeps it alive. For ways students can check in on goals, see pages 63-64 in the *Developmental Designs 1 Resource Book.*

Salome, think about your math goal for this year as you work on these problems, and be sure to ask for help if you need it.

Shannon, what social goal did you set in advisory? ("I will be more assertive.") What will you do to meet that goal today during our class discussion?

Damone, you want to be a rapper. This means you have to have interesting things to say and rhythm in your language. Let's look at this piece of writing for both.

Weekly self-assessment

At a school in Vermont, an advisory group created "goals in a jar." On small pieces of paper, students set realistic, short-term goals each Monday in advisory and put them in a jar. At the end of the week, they take turns pulling goals out of the jar and reading them aloud. The student who wrote the goal shares what s/he did to reach the goal and how close s/he came to reaching it, and s/he and/or classmates may say what might have been a barrier or a builder in accomplishing the goal. The class does a quick cheer or acknowledgment for the student before the next goal is pulled from the jar and read. The authors of goals provide evidence to show how successful s/he has been. See the article *Coaches' Corner: Goals in a Jar* by Scott Tyink at the *Developmental Designs* Web site for the complete process.

At another school, students write a brief letter home each Friday describing their progress toward goals and how well they abided by the Social Contract during the week.

Another way to keep goals alive is through weekly journal reflection. Students respond to specific focus questions like:

Action steps: What specific action steps did you take this week toward your goal?

Obstacles: What obstacles got in your way this week?

Next steps: What remains to be done to reach your goal?

Similar questions could be responded to on Exit Cards (students hand in responses written on cards as they leave class) or in a partner share at the end of a period or a week, keeping students' goals present. Because choice boosts engagement and relevance, have students choose their questions whenever possible. The process doesn't have to take long, but it needs to occur regularly to nurture a lively connection to goals.

Keeping the rules alive

A feeling of accomplishment permeates the community when they reach consensus, and Social Contracts are often posted with fanfare and acknowledgment of the considerable effort and compromise that brought it into being. Next comes the day-to-day work of abiding by the Contract through thick and thin. The key is for students to have the Contract be the foundation for behavior choices. Likewise, you must have it be the basis on which you enforce the rules. In this way, among other benefits, you shift some of your authority to the group who created and endorsed the Contract. Instead of *I want you to...*, refer to the group's declaration: *We have agreed...* or *Our rules say....*

Resources:

- See article *Social Contract: An Underused Developmental Designs Practice* by Scott Tyink at www.DevelopmentalDesigns.org

- See article *Coaches' Corner: Keeping the Social Contract Alive* by Scott Tyink at www.DevelopmentalDesigns.org

- See how one teacher tended the rule like she tends her garden in the article *Cultivating and Celebrating the Rules,* by Traci Lynse at www.DevelopmentalDesigns.org

Take the Contract seriously

The Social Contract is your bulwark for behavior management. It is the declaration of standards and expectations, created and endorsed by teachers and students, to which everyone must be held accountable. Try a think-aloud with students to demonstrate how it will work:

If Inga pops her gum, is that a violation of the Social Contract? Let's look at our Contract. It says: Try your hardest, be respectful, and stay focused. Gum-popping isn't respectful because it creates a disruption for others. So, according to the Contract, Inga needs to stop popping her gum.

You might say: *Inga, check the Social Contract, please,* or *Inga, check the Contract and determine whether popping your gum aligns with it,* or, *Inga, you need to stop popping your gum. Our Social Contract says 'be respectful,' and gum-popping is not respectful.* Any of these could work, depending on the type of learner Inga is. The point is to invoke the Social Contract regarding a specific behavior. In this way, the central voice of authority is the Contract everyone created and endorsed, not just you. With power sourced democratically, students' pushback reflex may be diluted or defused.

Acknowledge positive use of the Contract

From time to time, acknowledge that students have abided by the Contract, so the rules aren't exclusively associated with misbehavior. Consider reflecting on the Social Contract at the end of a class period. Ask open-ended questions that recognize and acknowledge success: *Which rule did you abide by today when you could have broken it? What is one rule you noticed your partner following today?* Ask students to support their answers with evidence.

Resources:

- For longer acknowledgment activities and quick cheers, see *Developmental Designs 1 Resource Book*, pages 185-187

- See how one teacher linked positive behavior to the Contract in the article *Bringing the Social Contract to Life in the Classroom* by Matthew Christen at www.DevelopmentalDesigns.org

Assume nothing, teach everything

Some students might agree to and mean to abide by the Social Contract, but lack the skills to do so. Appropriate behavior must be taught through modeling and practicing, including responding to redirection. Likewise, you must practice consistent, fair redirection for everyone. See in this *Guide* Teacher Preparation sections in Strategies for Modeling and Practicing and Strategies for Pathways to Self-control.

Use the Loop

At the core of the shift from "what's good for me" to "what's good for the group" is the skill of self-control. Help students develop this skill and an understanding of its importance through the plan/reflect cycle of the Loop. Use the Loop as you teach and establish routines and to teach awareness of appropriate and/or rule-breaking behavior.

Resource: See the *Developmental Designs 1 Resource Book*, pages 6-7, for examples of using the Loop for routines and lesson protocols.

Acknowledge accountability

A positive way to help students keep the rules in mind is to end class once a week with an acknowledgment that invokes the Social Contract. Have students recall an act of kindness they noticed during the week. Next, have them read the rules in the Social Contract and mentally connect the act of kindness to one or more of the rules. Finally, one at a time, volunteers say, *I acknowledge [classmate] for demonstrating [rule in the Contract] when she [behavior].* For example, *I acknowledge Elizabeth for showing respect when she caught a moth and let it out through the window,* or *I acknowledge Pedro for volunteering to read his poem when no one wanted to go first.*

ENDORSEMENT

Check *your* endorsement of the Social Contract

Like most people, students value and respect rules more if they feel ownership of them. This is the power of democracy: a Social Contract created and endorsed by everyone that can lead to an orderly classroom and an orderly school, free of threats, bribes, rewards, and punishment. If you are not sure you endorse this collaborative process, review the premise of the Social Contract on page 73 in *Classroom Discipline* and pages 65-66 in the *Developmental Designs 1 Resource Book*.

Resource: See about positive behavior gains resulting from a school-wide Contract in the article *School-Wide Social Contract* by Mark Carbone at www.DevelopmentalDesigns.org

Student Endorsement

If some students balk at the rule-creating process, pose the alternative as a point of discussion: *Would you rather have the adults decide on the rules and just tell you what they will be, or do you want to have a say?* Chances are they will choose the latter.

Key to *ongoing* student endorsement is daily use of the Contract. After the hard work of creating and endorsing it, reflecting on the rules everyone created—how they guide us, how they affect our choices, how they show up positively day to day—shows your respect for the Contract and allows students to refresh their endorsement. There are more ideas for keeping the Contract alive in Accountability, above.

Hope, goals, and growth mindset

Your effective introduction of the goal-setting and rules-creation process is key to student interest and buy-in. Be sure the spark (page 76 above) is interesting and inspiring. It should connect to a trait related to goal achievement, like perseverance, resilience, or willingness to delay gratification. Your choice for the artistic display of student goals also matters: it should express seriousness of purpose and appeal to students. It's important to select sparks and creative displays that don't strike students as the much dreaded babyish.

Some students may not be familiar with hope, and some may have failed to reach goals in the past. Tell everyone that in this classroom, hope lives, and tell them you will work with them to reach their goal. If a student still won't declare a goal, suggest one based on what you know: *You have a strong, unique voice, Denzel. Getting good at expressing yourself in writing would be a meaningful and interesting goal for you this year, and I would like to help you accomplish it. What do you think?*

The voice of your growth mindset tells the student that you believe in his capacity for growth and will help him overcome barriers. See Chapter Two: Mindsets Create the Tone of Teaching for a detailed discussion of fostering a growth mindset.

One school increases Contract endorsement through participation. They direct students at the beginning of the year to identify the most important routines needed to support the Contract and then develop look/sound/feel charts in small groups.

"Play" with the rules

Students can increase their mastery and endorsement of the rules by

- creating a sung version of the Social Contract

- creating a skit or role play about positively observing the rules

- adapting and/or playing games from the *Developmental Designs 2 Resource Book* such as Parkbench, page 175, The Great Brain, page 172, and Freeze Frame, page 171, to explore the rules

- creating public service announcements or posters promoting the rules. When they are complete and of high quality, follow through by airing or posting them.

Creating safety for goal setting

Sharing goals helps build a community of learners and broadens the base of support for reaching the goals, but some students simply may not want to share their goals with their peers (for the moment, we hope). You may allow a student to share only with you. Tell her or him that you hope this is a temporary solution.

Sharing goals with a partner rather than with the whole class might ease concerns about safety early in the year. You might display envelopes containing the goal declarations, so they are part of the environment and near the Social Contract, but private. Finally, you could read the goals aloud, omitting names, or let students choose whether to have their names read.

Involving families

You may wish to send goal-setting information home to families and ask them to create a goal together. These could be incorporated into student goals for display.

Resource: See a family goal-setting recording sheet in the *Developmental Designs 1 Resource Book*, page 62.

ENGAGEMENT

Varied methods for gathering Contract input

If students don't actually resist the idea of the Contract but seem bored or uncertain in the process, it could be that the method of gathering input is not clear enough or lively or safe for everyone. Use a variety of routines for managing conversations so everyone is included. Be clear about what method you are using; taking the mystery out of when and how student voices are heard reduces anxiety. If the process is lengthy, take breaks, use energizers, and consider continuing another day. Mix up where students sit, and have them take the roles of timekeeper and recorder.

Resources:

- Managing Conversations resources in Educator Help at www. DevelopmentalDesigns.org

- See how one teacher uses engaging, relevant activities to generate the Social Contract in the article *Words to Guide Actions* by Christopher Hagedorn at www.DevelopmentalDesigns.org

Sometimes, raising expectations boosts engagement. Put older students in charge of running rule-creation meetings with younger students. See how one teacher nurtured student leadership in advisory in the *Developmental Designs 1 Resource Book*, page 47, and consider translating this to the Contract process.

Reflect on the degree of your follow-through with the rules. The most common source of student disengagement is when students perceive the process as a waste of time.

Vary sparks and displays for recording goals

If students seem to value goal setting in school but don't engage, perhaps your process needs adjustment. Students can become bored if the same spark appears year after year, or if they use the same recording sheet in every class. Use the arts to enliven displays and to explore the meaning of the rules. Expressing goals and rules through collage, poetry, skits, and photographs is unfailingly enlivening.

Resource: See *Gecko Tessellations: Goals and Declarations Display* at www.DevelopmentalDesigns.org for a creative goal-display process

---

1 Ontario Ministry of Education, Canada, "Aboriginal Perspectives: A Guide to the Teacher's Toolkit," page 8, http://www.edu.gov.on.ca/eng/aboriginal/Guide_Toolkit2009.pdf.

CHAPTER FIVE

Modeling and Practicing

REFLECTING ON MODELING AND PRACTICING

BARRIERS TO MODELING AND PRACTICING

STRATEGIES FOR MODELING AND PRACTICING

REFLECTING ON MODELING AND PRACTICING

Activate your *growth mindset* as you consider this vision for setting clear expectations collaboratively with students for the daily routines and procedures. Reflect on the degree to which you engage best practice. Even in the strongest practice, there is always room for growth. Even in a beginning practice, there is always evidence of strength. Take stock, then select what you want to work on.

1. **Use of the modeling format:** Do I use the steps in the modeling process (goal, ideas from students, student/teacher demonstrations, noticing and questioning, practice, and discussion of what-ifs)?

2. **Target behavior and payoffs:** Do all students know the target behavior for the routine and understand the benefits of following expectations in a positive manner?

3. **Student participation:** During the modeling process, do students contribute ideas for the routine or procedure?

4. **Student demonstrations:** Are students willing to demonstrate the expected behavior when appropriate (when the routine or procedure is familiar enough)?

5. **Student noticing and questioning:** Do students notice expected behaviors during demonstrations in response to my open-ended questions?

6. **Visual reminders:** Do students and I create effective visuals to support a routine or procedure?

7. **Follow-up practice:** Do all students have opportunities to practice the expected behavior until they have mastered it?

8. **Follow-up reflection:** Do I periodically invite students to reflect on our success with a routine?

9. **Follow-up adjustments:** When a routine begins to slip, do I respond with appropriate interventions (remodel, remind, ask a reflection question, redo, refer to visual agreements)?

10. **Follow-up reinforcement:** When the routine is going well, do I recognize the group's positive behavior with reinforcing language, an acknowledgment, or a cheer

BARRIERS TO MODELING AND PRACTICING

Identify barriers

What's getting in the way when you model and practice routines and procedures? Review what other teachers identify as barriers to growth. Keeping in mind the element of modeling and practicing you've selected to work on, identify the following common barriers to growth that fit your experience.

Identify strategy areas

The barriers are grouped into the six strategy areas: Relationship, Teacher Preparation, Expectations, Accountability, Endorsement, and Engagement. Identify the strategy area most relevant to your experience. For example, if barriers described under Relationship reflect what you observe in students or yourself, start by reading that Strategies section on page 90.

Common Barriers to Growth

Relationship

Students resist modeling and seem to experience it as primarily teacher control. Lack of trust hampers student participation in the modeling process.

Teacher Preparation

I am unclear about or forgot the modeling and remodeling steps.

I am unclear about which intervention(s) to use when students do not follow expectations for routines.

I am unclear how to use reflection to support a routine.

There isn't enough time to model or follow all the steps (e.g., getting student input).

I need more ideas and planning time for modeling (a list of routines to model, schedule of when to model, ideas for teacher language).

I need ideas for engaging students in creating visual reminders to help students learn and remember a routine.

Expectations

Behavior disruptions often hamper the modeling process.

My students don't yet have the skills necessary to successfully complete the routine.

Students seem more interested when I model the *wrong* way, so I do that first.

Accountability

Students know the routine, but I am not always able to hold them to the expectations set in the modeling.

We do not have enough time for students to practice the routine to increase competency.

I need more ideas for using the visual reminders effectively to keep students accountable. I tend to take them down too quickly or forget about them.

Students followed expectations for a while but now the routine is slipping.

Endorsement

Students balk at modeling and practicing and say it's childish.

Students do not understand the benefits of doing the routine or procedure in a positive manner.

Students do not want to talk or hear about the importance of setting expectations.

I do not see the value of modeling and practicing or of some of the steps (e.g., demonstrating).

Visual reminders take more time to create than they are worth.

Engagement

Students seem bored during the modeling process.

Students are reluctant to offer input or to demonstrate during modeling.

Students do not seem to have ideas to contribute.

STRATEGIES FOR MODELING AND PRACTICING

The strategies are organized into six areas: Relationship, Teacher Preparation, Expectations, Accountability, Endorsement, and Engagement. Follow these steps to make the most of the detailed suggestions provided:

1. Read Chapter Two: Mindsets Create the Tone of Teaching as context for all the strategies.
2. Read the strategies areas identified by your review of Barriers to Modeling and Practicing.
3. Follow suggestions and your interest to read other, related areas.

General resources

Find specific resources are referenced throughout the strategies, e.g., a grid of activities or article about creating endorsement. Explore the following *Developmental Designs* resources for additional, detailed support for modeling and practicing:

- *Developmental Designs 1 Resource Book*
- *Developmental Designs 2 Resource Book*
- *The Advisory Book: Building a Community of Learners Grades 5-9*
- *Classroom Discipline: Guiding Adolescents to Responsible Independence*
- *The Circle of Power and Respect Advisory Meeting* DVD
- *Modeling and Practicing Classroom Routines* DVD
- www.DevelopmentalDesigns.org (free articles, meeting content, and other resources)
- http://www.YouTube.com/user/DevelopmentalDesigns (see practices in action)

RELATIONSHIP

Mindsets are Key

We model procedures and routines with students to help them grow in autonomy and competence and to expedite the learning process. Skipping the step of establishing clear expectations risks student confusion and forcing the teacher to do more management.

When we model with students, we need to make clear to them the importance of the practice. We may need to work through resistance, shifting their perception from dominance/submission to collaboration. The three teacher mindsets help immensely.

Growth mindset

Modeling calls on students to play a role in their own behavior management. Taking student input seriously at each step of the modeling process, you reinforce your belief in students' capacity for growth, and students experience their capacity for maturity in what is usually an entirely teacher-controlled realm of learning: how we will do things. *I know your creativity and experience will help shape an efficient process and I know your maturity will help you follow through.*

Action mindset

Taking the time to model demonstrates your willingness to do what it takes to support student autonomy and competence. And if it's worth your time, it's worth theirs: *You know I don't treat you like babies. I expect a lot of you. By setting and practicing these expectations together, you share in the responsibility for how these go in the classroom. My job always includes holding everyone accountable to whatever the expectations we define.* Your action mindset communicates your confidence in the value of the process and in students to participate and master it: *Getting it right will save us quite a bit of time for the rest of the year, and we won't have to talk about it. Who will help me model this?*

Objective mindset

Somebody said this process treats you like babies, but I don't think so. When an adult is hired for a new job, there is a period of training, in which they are shown how to do the job and they practice it and ask questions for clarification. They know they will be held accountable for their performance, and this is their opportunity to fully understand the expectations for the job. Compare students to adults, not to the babies they are so concerned to not be! Your objective mindset shows that the process is not about them, it is what creates an environment for everyone's success.

See more about how to establish the importance of modeling with students under Endorsement, page 95, and Expectations, page 94

Clear Expectations Strengthen Teacher-student Relationships

Adolescents thrive in strong, healthy relationships and supportive communities. Modeling strengthens teacher-student relationships by respecting students' autonomy and competence: once a routine is established, students operate with growing independence and skill. Modeling fosters supportive communities by making expectations clear and explicitly aligning them with the Social Contract everyone has endorsed.

Set the stage for endorsement

Students need to see the connection between clear expectations and their own growth in autonomy and competence. Modeling is a tool for their learning and growth, not for teacher dominance. Try creating hypothetical situations, visions of learning with and without clear expectations, as a community and individually:

Think about traffic. Signs, stoplights, lines and lanes, barriers and emergency lights all maintain order so accidents are less likely and drivers reach their destinations as safely and efficiently as possible. What would traffic be like without the signs and lines and lanes? [Class discusses briefly] *It's the same for our classroom, except we have far fewer rules than there are for driving. Clear rules and cooperation with them help everyone learn and grow safely and efficiently.*

Share your vision

Modeling reflects your intention and hope that all students will succeed in school. Say so. Efficient routines save time and energy for exploring ideas and developing skills instead of redoing, repeating, or repairing. They make it easy to show respect for the learning community by operating according to clear expectations everyone endorsed.

Rules and expectations can be rungs on a ladder or bars on a door. In jail, the rules are bars on the door, designed to keep people confined. In school and in our classroom, they are rungs on the ladder that leads to your success in life. One step at a time, with effort and care, you rise. I'm here to steady the ladder for you, to teach and encourage and guide, and to tell you when you've taken a misstep, and help you get both feet back on the ladder.

Build trust in the community to encourage participation

The *Developmental Designs* process of modeling is collaborative. It calls on students to offer input, to volunteer to demonstrate acceptable behavior, and to reflect on the benefits of the routine. The community needs to endorse the process and participation in it. You may need to start slowly and demonstrate the behavior yourself until the community supports risk-taking. Respond consistently and decisively to any put-downs of students who participate.

Consider starting with a two-minute game to relax and build community. The fun, laughter, and bit of vulnerability will generate trust and a culture of participation.

Resource: For games that can fit into the flow of a busy class period, see *The Advisory Book* chart on pages 213-215 and look at those labelled "quick."

TEACHER PREPARATION

There are five steps to the modeling process: Ideas from Students, Demonstration, Noticing, Practice, and What-ifs. Each step includes input from students. We take the same steps when we try a new recipe or learn to drive.

Resources: To review modeling steps, see *Classroom Discipline*, pages 89-91, or the *Developmental Designs 1 Resource Book*, pages 70-73.

Who will demonstrate the routine?

Students may be able to demonstrate the routine during the modeling process; this is great, since it empowers those who do the modeling, and it probably lowers others' resistance. The teacher needs to model routines that require knowledge or skills that students don't know yet.

List routines that need to be modeled and when

Refer to lists on pages 79-80 in the *Developmental Designs 1 Resource Book* for ideas. Mentally scan your class periods and ask yourself what routines are necessary to support instruction and student learning, and which should take precedence. Then plan the sequence.

During the first six weeks of school, keep things simple: have students use just a few materials and procedures, and slowly increase the complexity of both. Think about the complexity of routines. Perhaps during the first few weeks you will appoint a student to collect homework, and a little later introduce the routine of handing in homework.

If you are part of a team, plan before the start of the school year who will model what and when during the first few weeks of school. This ensures that all essential routines get modeled, and it avoids repetition for students.

Resource: Read about steps teams can take together to create consistent classroom and school-wide routines in the article *Teaming for Success* by Christopher Hagedorn at www.DevelopmentalDesigns.org.

Write out the steps

It can be helpful to write out the steps of a routine before modeling with students. This increases your comfort and clarity with the process and helps you anticipate potential trouble spots to address. It can also help you identify anything problematic about the routine itself, such as complexity or the order of steps.

You can write a script for the modeling demonstration, including key questions you want to ask students during the process. Use the planning sheet for introducing a routine in the *Developmental Designs 1 Resource Book,* page 81. Have the script handy while you model the routine with students. Teachers report that they quickly integrate the process into their teaching and gain confidence and comfort quickly after following this rigorous introduction the first few times.

Resource: Learn how one teacher built an efficient routine for entering the classroom by modeling it in small parts in the article *Modeling and Practicing Routines to Improve Behavior* by Nancy Pulkrabek at www.DevelopmentalDesigns.org.

Enlist student help in creating visual reminders

Review the examples of visual reminders on pages 74-75 of the *Developmental Designs 1 Resource Book,* then get students involved in creating these supports. As participation in this step increases, so does endorsement of modeling and practicing. Invite students to invent graphic organizers other than the usual Y-chart, T-chart, and lists, and use student-generated materials and strategies when you can.

Plan follow-up support

Follow-up is essential after the initial modeling to help students gain competence with the routine. If the routine is new and/or complex, expect students to forget some steps or details at first and to need follow-up support. Follow-up strategies include reflection about how the routine is working, referring back to any visuals you created to support the routine, and practical adjustments to the routine. See details about these strategies in Accountability, below on page 97.

The never-ending Loop

Prepare some open-ended questions for reflection and planning with students after the modeling process. Here are some starters:

- What went well today when we...?
- What do we need to do differently the next time we...?
- How can we make_____ more efficient?
- What did you notice about the way we...?

EXPECTATIONS

Modeling is the way we usually set expectations. In the first few weeks of school, though, it's possible that modeling is hampered because you can't keep students' attention long enough. To maximize effective communication at first:

- keep things brief and moving along—the shorter, the better
- use as few words as possible
- engage students by seeking input and having them demonstrate; be sure they have time to ask clarifying questions
- tell students at the outset how long you think the modeling will take
- require and practice hand-raising so blurts don't happen.

Reinforce why modeling is necessary

Use strategies suggested above in Relationship, page 90, and below in Endorsement, page 95, to establish with students the purpose for modeling. Once they see the value of the process, they can support it: *I imagine most of you have some experience moving furniture. Here, we must do it in a crowded room, quickly. We'll draw on your experience and insights to make a clear plan, and then we'll follow it all year.*

Use visuals to clarify expectations

Some students need a visual reminder. A picture or list of the routine's steps posted in the room for a few weeks for them to refer to might help them recall and internalize the routine, especially if they create it or help do so. See examples of visual reminders on pages 74-75 in the *Developmental Designs 1 Resource Book*.

Resource: Read ways to maximize the use of visual reminders in the article *Coaches' Corner: Skillful Use of Visual Reminders* by Christopher Hagedorn, at www.DevelopmentalDesigns.org.

Match expectations to students' skills

Sometimes you learn in the course of modeling and practice that students do not yet have all the skills necessary for the routine. Perhaps you can modify or postpone teaching the routine. For example, if a routine requires partnering and your students haven't practiced pairing up, you can practice that skill, then return to modeling the routine you started with.

You may need to adjust your expectations for how long it will take your students to learn the routine after the initial modeling. See Accountability/Modeling is just the beginning, below on page 97.

ENDORSEMENT

Review *your* endorsement

To reinforce your belief in the benefit of modeling consider how you form a new habit or learn a routine. Chances are you seek input and especially appreciate learning through demonstration (Input and Demonstration). You always need a chance to notice what works, then practice (Notice and Practice), and possibly double-back to problem solve the sticky spots (What-ifs). Note the parallels to the modeling process in parenthesis.

Resource: Read one teacher's reflections on the long term benefits of modeling to academic learning in the article *Taking Our Time* by Ann Larson Ericson at www.DevelopmentalDesigns.org.

Discuss the need for clear expectations

The first step for successful modeling is for everyone to affirm the need for expectations. Most adolescents want as few rules as possible, and many openly or furtively rebel against or sabotage expectations they feel are unnecessary. Such rebellion is even more likely when rules and expectations are simply imposed on them. Taking the time to discuss the value of setting expectations, then going through a process that involves everyone in setting and endorsing clear expectations, shows respect for students' need for autonomy and competence. See an example analogy on page 91, under Relationship/Set the stage for endorsement.

Ask authentic, open-ended questions:

Why create routines? Why set expectations for them?

What might happen if we don't have clear expectations?

Is there a routine that seems too simple to require modeling or setting expectations?

Why does the expectation for even this simple routine need to be clear to all?

Can you think of a time when you learned something by watching rather than being told about it?

Why do we model expectations?

Tell stories about life with and without expectations

Share a story about a time when your success was compromised by lack of routine or expectation. Ask students to reflect on their lives with and without expectations:

Are there times or situations outside of school where you set and/or follow expectations?

Are there times or situations outside of school where you think things would go better if there were clear expectations?

Clear expectations help people accomplish great things

Tell a story from history or your own experience about how individuals or groups guided by clear expectations have accomplished great things. For example, the young people who joined the civil-rights movement were taught and held to very demanding expectations for their behavior under extreme pressure. And athletes who perform at the highest levels—Olympians and champions—adhere to the constricting but clear expectations of their coaches. You are a good coach for your students' social and academic success.

Take on the "too simple or babyish" issue

Some students will feel that some routines are too simple to warrant time for modeling and practicing. *Why do we need a routine for simply entering the classroom? I don't have a routine for entering my bedroom!* Ask students to consider the routine in the context of a busy classroom with students moving about and trying to get work done. Then routines that may seem simple become more complex, and are essential for a positive environment where everyone can be successful. Cooperating in using routines is a way of collaborating in our work.

Taking perspective

Ask students to consider arguments *for* setting expectations, especially when a routine may seem too simple to require modeling:

Why might the seemingly simple routine of gathering homework at the start of class require setting expectations? Why might you appreciate a routine for this ordinary exchange in our class?

I respect your competence. I believe gathering homework will be more efficient and successful if you watch it being modeled. If you had to defend my point of view, what would you say?

The power of demonstration

Ask student to recall a time when they learned something new by watching rather than just listening to or reading instructions. Ask how the demonstration helped and if they could have learned it without it.

Compare these experiences with classroom routines: *A quick demonstration of the way to turn in homework will eliminate the traffic jam that wastes our time and attention.*

Always model the *correct* procedure, *never* an incorrect one, because of the power of demonstration. Students may find it entertaining to see you acting inappropriately, but they also are committing it to memory.

Solicit student input

Student endorsement of the routine you model is built into the modeling steps. See pp 73 of the *Developmental Designs 1 Resource Book* or pp. 89-91 in *Classroom Discipline*. Step One, Eliciting Ideas from Students, implicitly invites their endorsement:

Why is it important to…. Why is it to your advantage to be able to do this well? They describe the main characteristics of the routine in Step Three, when the teacher asks, *What did you notice?* and students respond. This addresses their need for autonomy and competence.

Explain the long view

Help students see that mastering routines early in the year will allow for more autonomy and flow later in the year: "We're taking things slowly now so we can get our systems in place and can learn more and move faster later in the year." Aphorisms abound that assert the wisdom of setting expectations: An ounce of prevention is worth a pound of cure; the devil is in the details, so let's get the details down; an apple a day helps keep the doctor away, and so on.

Involve students in assessment

In addition to the initial modeling demonstration including students, students should participate in assessing the routine. You could ask one student per day to share his/her opinion of how well s/he thinks they fulfilled class expectations for the routine, or you could set goals together for progress (i.e. cleanup will take two minutes), and find an engaging way to keep track (i.e. a graph or chart created and updated by students).

ACCOUNTABILITY

Modeling is only the beginning

Modeling allows for rigorous accountability. This begins with full participation in the modeling. Use strategies offered under Relationship, Expectations, and Endorsement to maximize participation and understanding from the start. After the modeling process, it will take a lot of practice to establish a habit, so don't give up if your students don't catch on immediately after the modeling. According to a 2011 study, the median time it took a person to learn a new habit was 66 days.[1]

Practice doesn't need to take a lot of time. Whenever the class employs the routine, have them briefly reflect on how successful it was. Make additional practice fun by setting out challenges, like doing it faster or more quietly. Better yet, have the students create the challenge.

Resource: Learn how teachers used modeling and practicing and other strategies to maintain a strong signal for attention in the article *Reviving the Silence for Attention* at www.DevelopmentalDesigns.org.

Remodel after a break

The whole group can benefit from a quick remodel of routines after breaks from school. When the routine is first being established, remodeling on Mondays may be necessary. Even a two-day break can displace school routines. The key to remodeling is to keep it short and acknowledge that students already know the steps of the routine but would benefit from a quick review.

Take action as soon as the routine starts slipping

As soon as you notice that a routine is practiced somewhat carelessly, ask yourself whether a remodel is in order or whether something else (e.g. Stop and Think Modeling, visual reminder check-in, or the Loop) might be useful. Your choice is an important part of planning, and it depends on several factors, including how often or recently you've already modeled it, what else you've tried to correct the routine, etc. The following sections address some options for action.

Determine whether this is a group or individual issue

The group will likely resent being led through a remodeling when only a few are messing up. The strategies addressed in this section are appropriate for individuals, small groups, and whole classes, depending on who is/are struggling.

Never nag! Use the Loop

The Loop leads students into reflection on behavior, then appropriate corrective action, and it prevents you from nagging when you see things slipping. Ask students to check in on the routine: *Let's check in. What did you notice about that transition? What can we do to fix it?* This communicates that you saw what happened, and it has to be fixed, but you will not micromanage the routine. It is their responsibility.

Remodel if the whole group seems unclear

Remodeling is called for when the whole group or nearly the whole group seems unclear about the routine's steps. This is different from practice, whose purpose is to make the routine a habit. The purpose of remodeling is to quickly review protocol and see the demonstration again. If your students don't need this clarification, then allow more time for practice and reflection.

Resource: Review remodeling steps in *Classroom Discipline*, pages 107-109.

Refer back to visuals

Refer back to visuals created when the routine was first established:

- Remind me how we agreed our cleanup should look, sound, and feel.
- Which steps did we do well? Which gave you trouble?

You may need to create new visuals to support certain students. If all of your visuals rely on words, create one that includes hand-drawn pictures or photos. An image of students doing the routine with success can be a reminder of the expectations.

Use Stop and Think Modeling

Stop and Think Modeling is a variation of the modeling steps that helps students address problematic issues that occur during routines, such as being late for class or finding a spot in the circle when all seats are taken. It is a lively and engaging way to have students think about positive solutions and then practice by dramatizing the situation.

Resource: See Stop and Think Modeling directions in *The Advisory Book*, pages 113-114.

ENGAGEMENT

If students appear detached from or bored by the modeling process, assess their understanding of the "why" and "how" of the practice. This could make the difference between an experience that seems meaningless and one that is understood as an expression of respect and commitment to learning. Find strategies to increase engagement under Relationship, Endorsement, and Expectations.

Increase variety and student input

Adolescents can start to tune out; engage them with variety and with participation in the process. Appoint one or more students to time the routine and report to the class, or invite students to make a poster that will help everyone remember the steps of the routine.

There is almost always more than one good way to do a routine. The point is that the routine should support learners and the learning environment. In your first modeling, be open to a few students' different ways to do a routine (they must rise to the standards of safety and efficiency) e.g., two ways to carry chairs to form or disband a circle.

You can respond to a routine that is beginning to slip by asking students: *Does our routine still fit our community? Are we ready to do this differently because our skills have increased, or simply because we are ready for a change?* (Either is a valid reason)

Most adolescents love variety. Encourage engagement and creativity and build autonomy and competence by inviting students to invent a better way.

Resource: Read how one teacher used variety and responsiveness to create finely tuned signals for attention in the article *As Goes the Signal, So Goes the Class* by Kristen Konop at www.DevelopmentalDesigns.org.

Encourage student leadership

Are students ready for leadership roles in routines or in modeling? If a routine is timed, have a student be the timekeeper. If a routine involves a quality check, have a student be the checker. Have student demonstrators whenever possible. There are many ways to solicit student input, like drawing sticks or allowing one minute for a turn and talk on the topic before seeking input. The more you pass the power to the students, the more interesting the process will be for them.

---

1 D. T. Neal, W. Wood, J. S. Labrecque, and P. Lally, "How Do Habits Guide Behavior? Perceived and Actual Triggers of Habits in Daily Life," *Journal of Experimental Social Psychology* 48 (2012): 492-498.

CHAPTER SIX

Empowering Language

REFLECTING ON EMPOWERING LANGUAGE

BARRIERS IN EMPOWERING LANGUAGE

STRATEGIES FOR EMPOWERING LANGUAGE

REFLECTING ON EMPOWERING LANGUAGE

Activate your *growth mindset* as you consider this vision for using empowering language. Reflect on the degree to which you engage best practice. Even in the strongest practice, there is always room for growth. Even in a beginning practice, there is always evidence of strength. Take stock, then select what you want to work on.

1. **Tone:** Do I speak to students with a calm, respectful, neutral, and confident voice?

2. **Voiceovers:** When a student speaks, do I refrain from repeating what s/he says?

3. **Directing:** Do I give concise information and provide written instructions, especially for tasks requiring more than three steps?

4. **Directing:** Do I check for understanding before releasing students to work?

5. **Reinforcing:** Do I describe specific behaviors without judgment when reinforcing positive behaviors?

6. **Reminding:** Do I help students to remember and state the expected behavior by asking reminding questions?

7. **Reminding:** Do I use reminding language proactively (e.g., before students begin a new task) more often than reacting to unmet behavior expectations?

8. **Redirecting:** Do I positively say what a student who has broken a rule needs to do to get back on track, without judgment or sarcasm?

9. **Redirecting:** Do I state redirections in a non-negotiable way?

10. **Reflecting:** Do I prompt students to monitor their own progress toward goals—looking both back and forward?

11. **Reflecting:** Do I guide individuals and groups to examine the quality of their work—strengths and weaknesses—relative to clear expectations?

12. **Reflecting:** Do I ask students to show evidence as they self-assess?

13. **Reflecting:** Do I ask students to reflect on both the process and product of their learning?

14. **Balance between reinforcing and redirecting:** Do I use reinforcing language as much as or more than redirecting language?

15. **Avoiding disempowering language:** Do I avoid language that does not empower students, such as sarcasm, praise, manipulation, and guilt?

16. **Nonverbal communication:** Do I use nonverbal communication neutrally, without emotion?

17. **Nonverbal communication:** Do I introduce, model, and practice the nonverbal cues I use with students so they understand the purpose and appropriate response?

BARRIERS TO EMPOWERING LANGUAGE

Identify barriers

What gets in the way of using empowering language? Review what other teachers identify as barriers to growth. Keeping in mind the modeling and practicing element you've selected to work on, identify the common barriers to growth that fit your experience.

Identify strategy areas

The barriers are grouped into the six strategy areas: Relationship, Teacher Preparation, Expectations, Accountability, Endorsement, and Engagement. Identify the strategy area most relevant to your experience. For example, if barriers described under Teacher Preparation reflect what you observe in students or yourself, start by reading that Strategies section on page 108.

Common Barriers to Growth

Relationship

I get angry sometimes, and it shows.

I use praise and other rewards to build positive relationships and motivation with students.

Sometimes I abandon my neutral tone to maintain my authority with students.

I am concerned that students will interpret my use of reinforcing language as lacking authority.

Teacher Preparation

I don't always plan my instruction thoroughly, and I realize too late that more directions are needed.

I need to refresh my memory of the types of empowering language.

I don't know what I sound like in the classroom, and I don't know where to start.

I don't feel comfortable with the characteristics of empowering language—it feels awkward and unfamiliar to speak that way.

I need more ideas for each of the types of empowering language.

I need nonverbal cues to add to my repertoire.

There is not enough time for students to self-assess (reflect, show evidence, or monitor progress).

I need to break my habit of describing the rule-breaking behavior instead of the expected behavior.

I need ways to get students to speak in strong voices so I don't need to use voiceovers.

I redirect more but do not see enough opportunities to reinforce.

Students tune out some types of empowering language (e.g., reminding language).

I am concerned about reinforcing and redirecting language interrupting the work atmosphere of the classroom.

Expectations

I use voiceovers because students do not speak loud enough to be heard.

The expectations for responding to nonverbal cues are not clear.

Students already know how to respond to nonverbal cues without modeling.

Endorsement

I believe sarcasm, shame, judgment, praise, and/or manipulation are effective in some situations.

Students do not see the benefits of some nonverbal and verbal language.

I believe adding emotion to verbal or nonverbal language can be effective, such as giving a misbehaving student an "evil eye" or expressing my pleasure when a student works hard.

I redirect, but I do not see enough value in reinforcing.

I believe I should use a non-negotiable tone only for more serious misbehaviors.

I find reminding language most useful for reacting to rule breaking; I don't use it much before students make mistakes.

STRATEGIES FOR EMPOWERING LANGUAGE

The strategies are organized into six areas: Relationship, Teacher Preparation, Expectations, Accountability, Endorsement, and Engagement. Follow these steps to make the most of the detailed suggestions provided:

1. Read Chapter Two: Mindsets Create the Tone of Teaching as context for all the strategies.
2. Read the strategies areas identified by your review of Barriers to Empowering Language.
3. Follow suggestions and your interest to read other, related areas.

General resources

Find specific resources are referenced throughout the strategies, e.g., article about effective redirecting language. Explore the following *Developmental Designs* resources for additional, detailed support for empowering language:

- *Developmental Designs 1 Resource Book*
- *Developmental Designs 2 Resource Book*
- *The Advisory Book: Building a Community of Learners Grades 5-9*
- *Face to Face Advisories: Bridging Cultural Gaps in Grades 5-9*
- *Classroom Discipline: Guiding Adolescents to Responsible Independence*
- *The Circle of Power and Respect Advisory Meeting* DVD
- *Modeling and Practicing Classroom Routines* DVD
- www.DevelopmentalDesigns.org (free articles, meeting content, and other resources)
- http://www.YouTube.com/user/DevelopmentalDesigns (see practices in action)

Mindsets are Key

Empowering teacher language draws on the three *Developmental Designs* mindsets. We use speaking more than any other mode to guide student behavior, to motivate, and to provide clear instruction. All three mindsets are necessary for effective classroom communication.

Growth mindset

Your growth mindset keeps belief in the possibility for growth present in all circumstances, regardless of how predictable or hopeless things seem. When we use empowering language with students, we communicate our belief that they can grow, and we help them develop their skills to do so. You might have a fixed mindset about your own ability to control your emotions, e.g., *I get angry sometimes, and you can't fight nature,* or about your skills, e.g., *I'm not good at discipline.* But your growth mindset says, *I am working on controlling my emotions,* and *discipline is my growing edge.* The same is true for students: Saying, *Darrell, take a break and calm down,* communicates not only an explicit direction, but also the implicit belief that he can control his emotion. Saying, *Keisha, your math homework was done well and on time,* implicitly acknowledges her effort and competence.

Objective mindset

It never helps an escalating situation for an adult to show anger and frustration. An objective mindset allows you to communicate calmly and clearly when a student is upset and emotive. Empowering language helps you maintain emotional distance so you can respond to students without taking their behavior personally or getting irritated. Your objectivity communicates to the student and to the rest of the class that you will see to it that the rules the class formulated and endorsed will be enforced: *Marni, you must concentrate so you can get this lesson. Pick up your things and move to this table.*

Action mindset

Changing habits of language requires belief that developing empowering language will have a positive influence on the learning environment. We use an action mindset to stretch ourselves, to change our patterns even when we aren't certain we can do it. We can coach ourselves: *Even though it feels awkward, I'm going to use less redirecting language and more reinforcing language when I see positive behaviors.* (For example, *Eric, moving Celia's chair for her helped us get ready faster for lunch.* Or, *Janel, I heard you clearly all the way up here. Speaking up gets your message out!*) The expression of your action mindset communicates your awareness of the engagement and progress of each student.

Resources:

- *Classroom Discipline,* pages 20-28
- *Teacher Mindset Stories from the Classroom* by Keith Edmonds, an article at www.DevelopmentalDesigns.org

RELATIONSHIP

Teacher-student relationships benefit from your effective use of empowering language. Students see that you believe in their capabilities and that you treat them respectfully. They might interpret your objective mindset as an abundance of patience, or your action mindset as simply a positive attitude, but you will find that your hard work pays off in a calmer, more productive day for all, and much less stress for you.

A teacher who reinforces too much while redirecting too little may be seen by students as unwilling or unable to enforce the social Contract, while a teacher who redirects constantly and doesn't do enough reinforcement appears rigid and nagging. Using both redirection and reinforcement shows withitness—caring, concern, and responsiveness to every student and commitment to everyone's progress. You are moving them toward more intrinsic, less teacher-dependent motivation and self-control.

Resources:

- Read a principal's reflection on students' perception in the article *Principal Portraits: Notes on Communication* by Todd Bartholomay at www.DevelopmentalDesigns.org

- Read how one teacher's positive connections with students impacted their reception of her redirections in the article *I'm Not Yelling, I'm Redirecting* by Ann Larson Ericson at www.DevelopmentalDesigns.org

TEACHER PREPARATION

The five types of empowering language are Directing, Reinforcing, Reminding, Redirecting, and Reflecting. To review the characteristics of each type of language, see *Developmental Designs 1 Resource Book*, pages 88-103.

Increase noticing and reflecting

You may want more information to guide your growth in empowering language. Consider recording a class period so you can view your own teaching, or ask a colleague to observe and take notes in your room to help you identify language patterns. Tally the number of times you use each of the five types of empowering language in a class period, and note habits such as "um" and "like" that hamper communication.

You could journal daily about your language for a certain period of time. When you look back at your writing, what do you notice? Do you overuse one type of language and underuse another? Do certain people or situations trigger certain language? Does your language change significantly depending on the time of day or on the group you are working with? Gaining insight into your own behavior is always useful.

Enlist help from and empower students

Empowering language is not just for adults. For example, you can teach students to use reflecting language with each other when they share their work. When empowering language is the classroom norm, it's likelier that everyone will practice it.

Write out what you want to say

Write down reminders of language habits you want to employ, and keep them handy. Try writing words you want to use on something you keep with you—a clipboard or a planner, say—or post them on sentence strips on the wall. As you preview your lessons for the day, add open-ended reflection questions to support critical thinking.

Think through directions

The goal of directing language is to say enough for students to succeed in their work without saying too much. Being concise takes practice. The rigor that comes with aiming for the fewest, clearest words will strengthen your teaching and will lessen the amount of time your voice dominates the room. To that end, you could write down and post directions if there are more than three steps.

Instead of asking the vague "Any questions?" before students start their work, ask, "Who can tell us what we're about to do?" This allows a student to hold the floor for a moment and to practice speaking to the class, and it allows everyone to hear the directions once more, from a fellow student.

Replace verbal cues with nonverbal cues

Minimize verbal interruptions and increase autonomy; replace some common verbal cues with nonverbal versions, such as motioning "sit down" instead of verbally directing students to do so. You can do this gradually: do the nonverbal signal simultaneously with the words a few times, then drop the words and use the nonverbal cue only.

Find a good moment

A reinforcing comment might disrupt a lesson or the quiet work atmosphere you want to reinforce. It may be best to wait a few minutes. Redirection is most effective at the moment of infraction, but you might choose to finish a sentence or a thought before redirecting, unless safety demands an immediate response. Redirect as discreetly as possible: move close to the student you address and speak quietly.

Balance reminding and redirecting

Avoid overusing reminding language when things aren't going well. A balance between reminding and redirecting is important. When a firm redirect is needed, students often resent indirectness. The right balance between reminding and redirecting language varies from situation to situation, but keep in mind the distinction between the two, and don't use reminding language when redirection is needed.

When you remind, be sure to teach students how you expect them to respond: be sure they know that when you ask them a reminding question, you expect them to fix a mistaken behavior, and show them how to do so.

Resources:

- Read two teachers' top ten ways to deflect conflict before a student gets off track in the article *Language and Mindset for Effective Redirection* by Keith Edmonds and Bernie Blosky at www.DevelopmentalDesigns.org

- Read more about the differences between reminding and redirecting language in the *Developmental Designs 1 Resource Book*, pages 88-103

EXPECTATIONS

Expect students to speak up

Teachers often repeat students' words (usually loudly!) because they want to be sure the rest of the class heard the student. But the repetition detracts from students' autonomy, drawing attention back to the teacher. Adolescents are developing their identities, and it is important to allow them to speak with authority, so they grow in confidence and in their sense of verbal competence. Instead of repeating what they say, teach students the expectations for speaking clearly and audibly, then reinforce, remind, and redirect.

Don't forget the importance of fun: use games and activities that require students to speak clearly and in varying voices so they can practice, hear, and discuss voice level, tone of voice, and clarity (see I Sit in The Grass, No, No, No, Zumi, Zumi, and various CPR share formats at www.DevelopmentalDesigns.org). Following the activity, use the Loop to reflect on how well they used their voices, and help them see the connection to serious discussion.

Depending on the scale of the issue, you can engage the whole class or individual students in practicing speaking by choosing an object across the room and projecting their voice to reach the object. The class can use nonverbal cues to alert speakers that they are not audible, such as putting a hand to one's ear.

Expect evidence

Help students learn to self-assess meaningfully, avoiding superficial analysis: teach them to support their assessments with evidence. For practice, after students reflect and write down a grade for themselves on a simple task, ask them, "What's your evidence?" Then they write a sentence or two explaining their reasons for the grade. Supplying supporting evidence for the grade moves self-assessment from an emotional realm into a more objective context. Practicing on small tasks prepares students to self-assess on larger projects.

Teach verbal and nonverbal cues

Students are more likely to respond quickly and appropriately to your cues when they understand the purpose of each cue and your expectation for response. Timely and consistent redirection helps students realize that they will be held accountable. Once your expectations are clearly communicated, meet with individual students who seem to need extra coaching regarding a cue or some language. Review as necessary, then *hold them accountable* as you do everyone else.

ENDORSEMENT

Developmental Designs empowering language nurtures positive relationship, engagement, independence, and, ultimately, learning. "We have a tool ready at every moment to make or break our relationships with students: our language. In every encounter, the tone of our voices, body language, and words can build connection or dismantle it, can help or hinder the process of students becoming responsibly independent." (*Classroom Discipline*, page 30)

Our language is deeply entwined with our personal histories and cultures. It is hard to isolate and examine it, much less change it. Consider these common sticking points for teachers whose language patterns are not empowering for students.

Humor and sarcasm

Consider whether your sense of humor could sometimes diminish a student's sense of worth, or if it could sometimes confuse students about your intentions or belief in them. Humor can lighten the mood of the class and enrich and enliven a lesson, but never at the embarrassment or expense of a student or a group.

Regardless of intentions, sarcasm carries a very high risk of misunderstanding and/or hurt feelings, and it is simply not appropriate in school.

Reinforcement and reflection vs. judgment and praise

Avoid the temptation to give students broad strokes of criticism or praise. They need specific feedback about their work, and they probably need help using the Loop to assess their strengths and identify their growing edges.

One example: You like the fact that students entered the room quickly and quietly, and you might have an urge to say so. But to help them develop intrinsic motivation, it's better to correlate their behavior with the benefits to the community rather than with your appreciation:

Your quiet, orderly arrival may allow us time for a game at the end of class today.

Another example: You recognize growth in a student's writing skills, but rather than compliment her, you help her reflect on what she did to succeed in the assignment: *Your arguments clearly support your thesis. What are two things you did to make these connections?*

Resource: Read how one teacher tracked and acknowledged positive growth to greatly improve classroom routines in the article *From Scattered Unreadiness to Winning Teamwork* by Terence Wilson at www.DevelopmentalDesigns.org

Reinforce competence; use reminding language proactively

Reminding language addresses students' need for competence and autonomy. It sets everyone up for success, unlike criticizing someone who messes up. Prior to a routine or activity, a quick review of expectations reminds everyone of what they will be accountable for: *Who will remind us how to safely store the Bunsen burners?*

Sweat the small stuff

It takes courage and consistency to deal effectively with student misbehavior. A key principle of Pathways is to intervene right away, while mistakes are small. Consistent response to small infractions—every little thing—avoids most escalation of emotion and behavior.

Jeannine, do your arrival in the classroom over, this time in accordance with our Contract. James, take a break.

Resources: Find support for cultivating mindsets for effective discipline in:

- Chapter Two: Mindsets Create the Tone of Teaching
- *Classroom Discipline*, pages 20-28 and 135-191

Employ nonverbal cues

The beauty of nonverbal cues is that they allow you to communicate discreetly, avoiding embarrassment, and keep the focus on the work or activity at hand. And they reduce the dominance of the teacher's voice: a silent cue allows for autonomy and competence as students manage themselves with less direction from authority.

Enlist student partnership

You could share your language project with students: *Starting today, I am going to work on describing what I see you doing and not judging it. I want you to get good at being aware of and assessing your own behavior. You know or can review our Contract and expectations and measure your behavior against it.*

To reinforce the sense of partnership, you could invite students to note your use of judging language and describing language over a five-minute period from time to time and give you respectful feedback.

Teach the habit of reflection

Most teachers get into a habit of reminding students (*Remember to keep your voice down, Sam*), but there is great value for students in learning to reflect for themselves. Ask them to recall expectations and measure their own behavior: *Sam, what voice level will support our partner work?* There are times when simply naming exactly what needs to happen is best, but at other times, students can practice the Loop: thinking about their behavior, assessing its success or appropriateness, and planning a change, if necessary.

Resource: Use reflecting language to boost daily engagement in curriculum. Read how one teacher use planning, reflection, and a focus on metacognition to help students become interested in learning and more aware of their academic development in *Active Process Engages Learners* by Sarah Ibson at www.DevelopmentalDesigns.org.

CHAPTER SEVEN

Pathways to Self-control

REFLECTING ON PATHWAYS TO SELF-CONTROL

BARRIERS TO PATHWAYS TO SELF-CONTROL

STRATEGIES FOR PATHWAYS TO SELF-CONTROL

REFLECTING ON PATHWAYS TO SELF-CONTROL

Activate your *growth mindset* as you consider this vision for using Pathways to Self-control. Reflect on the degree to which you engage best practice. Even in the strongest practice, there is always room for growth. Even in a beginning practice, there is always evidence of strength. Take stock, then select what you want to work on.

1. **Fostering endorsement:** Introducing each Pathways redirection, do I foster student understanding and endorsement by telling stories, making connections to students' lives outside of school, and/or otherwise demonstrating the purpose and value of the tool?

2. **Modeling:** Introducing each new redirection, do I model the essential student response procedures and give students an opportunity to practice?

3. **Visual reminders:** Do I write and post expectations for student responses to redirections?

4. **Noticing:** Do I notice and respond appropriately to small infractions such as side conversations, slouching, blurting, pencil tapping, daydreaming, unauthorized use of electronics, etc.?

5. **Timely and for small things:** Do I intervene quickly when infractions are still minor to get students back on track to avoid escalation and minimize the need for further redirection?

6. **Individualized:** Do I match my response to what I know about the situation and a particular student's needs when he or she requires redirection?

7. **Equally weighted:** Do I use redirection cues (nonverbal cues, take a break, redirecting language, loss of privilege, fix it on the spot), and teach students to respond positively to each redirect?

8. **Non-punitive:** Do I teach students that my redirects are not intended as punishment, but rather are intended to teach and encourage self-management?

9. **Language:** Redirecting students, do I use words, tones, and nonverbal cues that are direct, neutral, and supportive?

10. **Analyzing behavior as needs-based:** Do I try to understand what need (relationship, competence, autonomy, fun) may be driving student behavior?

11. **Growth mindset:** Do I make sure that students know I believe they can grow to be responsible and independent?

12. **Nonverbal cues:** Do I use nonverbal communication to minimize interruptions and maximize discreetness with students who respond well to it?

    Student response: Do students respond by quickly getting back on track?

13. **Fix It on the Spot:** When it's appropriate, do I have students fix mistakes right in the moment?

    Student response: Do students fix mistakes quickly and get back on track?

14. **Loss of privilege, relevance:** When using loss of privilege, do I take away a privilege that is related to the rule-breaking behavior?

15. **Loss of privilege, restoration and learning:** When a student loses a privilege, do I restore the privilege as soon as I see the student is ready?

    Student response: After losing a privilege, do students respond by quickly getting back on track? After a privilege is returned, do students make appropriate use of it?

16. **Reminding language:** Do I use reminding language when students would benefit from thinking about successful behavior expectations?

    Student response: Do students respond to reminding language by quickly getting back on track?

17. **Redirecting language:** Do I use redirecting language when it appears students would benefit most from hearing exactly what they need to do to get back on track?

    Student response: Do students respond to redirecting language by quickly getting back on track?

18. **Take a break:** Do I use take a break (TAB) interchangeably with other redirects? For example, do I use it to intervene early, and for small misbehaviors, in the same way I might use a nonverbal cue or Fix It on the Spot?

19. **Take a break location:** Do I direct students to the TAB area in the room with the TAB chair facing the action (not turned toward the wall)?

    Student response: Do students move quickly and calmly to TAB, center themselves, get their thoughts together, and return to class without repeating?

20. **Take a Break, student initiated:** Do students initiate trips to TAB to self-regulate their behavior?

21. **TAB Out and Back:** Do I direct students to TAB Out and Back when I believe they would benefit from a short break away from the classroom to regain their self-control? For example, do I use it after multiple in-class redirects have proven insufficient or after a student's misbehavior is more than a minor infraction but does not warrant a trip to the office?

    Student response: Do students move to the designated classroom, discretely sit in the prepared chair, address their behavior with a written reflection, and return to class refocused on learning?

22. **TAB OUT and Back, quick conference:** Do I confer with a student returning from TAB Out and Back to be sure she knows what the problem was, has a plan to solve it, and can count on my support?

23. **Repair, student response:** When appropriate, do students offer an action apology to repair harm they have caused?

24. **Relationship-building conference:** Do I meet with all students to get to know them and understand how best to address their behavior—learn about what they like to do, any concerns they have, which redirection tools they'd prefer that I use with them, etc.?

25. **Quick conference:** Do I quickly confer with individuals when it seems they would benefit from a conversation with me that focuses on 1) identifying a problem, 2) creating a plan to solve the problem, 3) conveying my commitment to their success?

    Student response: Do students respond to quick conferences by quickly getting back on track?

26. **Full problem-solving conference:** When it appears any student would benefit from a full problem-solving conference, do I plan and initiate one and take care to follow the steps?

    Student response: Following a full conference, do students improve their behavior?

BARRIERS TO PATHWAYS TO SELF-CONTROL

Identify barriers

What gets in the way of effectively using Pathways to Self-control? Review what other teachers identify as barriers to growth. Keeping in mind the Pathways element you've selected to work on, identify the common barriers to growth that fit your experience.

Identify strategy areas

The barriers are grouped into the six strategy areas: Relationship, Teacher Preparation, Expectations, Accountability, Endorsement, and Engagement. For example, if barriers described under Expectations reflect what you observe in students or yourself, start by reading that Strategies section on page 127.

Common Barriers to Growth

Relationship

I tend to dislike or disconnect from students who disrupt class.

I tend to use one redirection for all students, without differentiation.

I don't think about what needs students are trying to meet with their behaviors.

Some or all students may not believe that I want to help and believe they can grow.

I don't use some of the strategies because I expect students will ignore me or push back.

Students ignore my redirections.

Teacher Preparation

I am unclear about or forgot how to use some or all of Pathways to Self-control (e.g., when to intervene; what constitutes a small infraction, fostering effective student-initiated TAB).

I need more ideas for how to consistently communicate a growth mindset to all students.

I need more ideas and planning time for introducing redirections to students.

I haven't found the time to develop and/or use all of the strategies in Pathways to Self-control.

My teacher language hampers the effectiveness of Pathways to Self-control strategies.

I'm not sure which redirection to use for certain students and situations.

My room arrangement doesn't allow for TAB or TAB Out and Back or noticing small rule-breaking.

The school schedule doesn't allow time to use Pathways—especially reflecting on what needs might be driving rule-breaking behavior.

It makes more sense to me to use Pathways strategies as a sequence with more intervention for bigger mistakes.

My school's discipline system contradicts many of the Pathways to Self-control strategies.

School-established consequences (detention, loss of recess or lunch time, Saturday School, etc.) are easier to use than Pathways strategies.

Expectations

Students go through the motions of a redirection but then repeat the behavior.

Students do not follow all or some of the redirection steps (e.g., they go willingly to TAB Out but disrupt that class when they arrive).

Accountability

I do not always catch the small things.

I do not respond to rule breaking in a timely and consistent manner.

There is so much rule breaking, I can't respond to every little thing.

I do not hold students accountable for the plans we create during the conference after TAB Out and Back.

Endorsement

I don't believe in "sweating the small stuff." I believe in choosing my battles and giving students a chance to self-correct.

I don't believe in the premise of teaching discipline to students. I think students should be disciplined.

Students do not endorse the benefits of some or all Pathways redirections.

Students see different redirections for different students as unfair.

Students see the redirections as punitive.

I see some aspects of Pathways redirections as punitive.

Students do not accept responsibility for their actions or believe they need to change their behavior.

Engagement

I forget to keep students engaged by using the Loop to reflect on regaining self-control.

I need ideas for stories and metaphors about redirection that will keep students interested in developing their self-management through Pathways.

I need more ideas and planning time for acknowledgments and cheers to reinforce positive behaviors.

Students use TAB and TAB Out and Back to get out of class.

I need help engaging students in problem-solving their behavior in conferences.

STRATEGIES FOR PATHWAYS TO SELF-CONTROL

The strategies are organized into six areas: Relationship, Teacher Preparation, Expectations, Accountability, Endorsement, and Engagement. Follow these steps to make the most of the detailed suggestions provided:

1. Read Chapter Two: Mindsets Create the Tone of Teaching as context for all the strategies.

2. Read the strategies areas identified by your review of Barriers to Pathways to Self-control.

3. Follow suggestions and your interest to read other, related areas.

General resources

Find specific resources are referenced throughout the strategies, e.g., an article about effective signals for attention. Explore the following *Developmental Designs* resources for additional, detailed support for Pathways:

- *Developmental Designs 1 Resource Book*

- *Developmental Designs 2 Resource Book*

- *The Advisory Book: Building a Community of Learners Grades 5-9*

- *Classroom Discipline: Guiding Adolescents to Responsible Independence*

- *The Circle of Power and Respect Advisory Meeting DVD*

- *Modeling and Practicing Classroom Routines DVD*

- www.DevelopmentalDesigns.org (free articles, meeting content, and other resources)

- http://www.YouTube.com/user/DevelopmentalDesigns (see practices in action)

RELATIONSHIP

All *Developmental Designs* practices are based on the premise that students are more successful when they have strong relationships with their peers and their teachers. Teamwork enhances healthy teacher-student relationships. The obedience/punishment dynamic is replaced by one of collaboration and mutual respect, accompanied by high expectations and clearly defined roles.

Mindsets are key

Use growth, action, and objective mindsets—each one in the right time and place—to keep your teacher-student relationships strong. The growth mindset facilitates assessment of how each student responds to cues, and it helps teachers select the redirection that is likely to be most effective for each student. The action mindset allows teachers to sweat the small stuff and intervene early, when infractions are still minor, so students can turn themselves around as autonomously as possible. The objective mindset helps teachers create a distance between themselves and a student who is upset or emotive so clear-minded thinking can prevail.

Resource: Read how one educator connects relationship building with creating collaborative, problem-solving mindset in the article *Increasing Equity with Relationship-based Behavior Management* by Terrance Kwame-Ross at www.DevelopmentalDesigns.org

Build strong teacher-student relationships

Positive, inclusive, trusting relationships underlie successful behavior guidance. Relationships between teachers and students, among students, and among adults influence every action we take to discipline students and help them grow. That is why keeping relationships intact and healthy is paramount. A huge help in this everlasting responsibility is using structures to shape life in school. Practiced well, Pathways to Self-control strengthens teacher-student relationships with every intervention and redirection. Pathways structures respect everyone's dignity, and they allow appropriate autonomy for students.

Relationship is created through language and through how we *be*—the climate we create for interactions. How can we choose tone, body language, and words to support positive relationships with students? Most broadly, we maintain a positive, effective teacher mindset. Throughout the day, we make a point of greeting each student as he/she enters class. Using Pathways, teachers are friendly, positive, and interested in all students. They have high expectations for all students' behavior which are not negotiable, because their foundation is the Social Contract the students created and endorsed. They intervene immediately when behaviors begin to slip.

Resource: Read one administrator's account of how an attendance liaison was able to connect with the young people whose behaviors he hoped to change in the article *Authority with Heart, Discipline with Care* by Todd Bartholomay at www.DevelopmentalDesigns.org

A rule of thumb

When you need to make a split-second decision about which redirection strategy to use with a student, ask yourself: *Which one would best help her grow?* This is a useful guide for much decision-making.

Reflect to know where you stand

Reflecting on your relationships with students may reveal areas that need to change for optimal student growth.

Think of a student you struggle with. Make a list of some of his positive aspects. Reflect on whether you acknowledge those characteristics with him. Does he know you see good in him?

Now think of a student you struggle with, and make a list of some of his negative habits. Write an opposite for each negative characteristic, and think about situations when this student behaves in a positive manner.

Think of a student you often redirect. Reflect on your relationship with him/her. Is it generally positive? What do you do to get to know him/her better? Fill out the student profile sheet to gather more information.

Everyone wins

Happy, relaxed students are less likely to break rules and more likely to be more motivated to learn. Playing together a little from time to time helps students learn to interact cooperatively with each other and allows you to connect positively with everyone. Play and other lively activities can release tension in the classroom before refocussing on the lesson.

Through play, we learn about others: who tends to lead or take charge, who is a clever detective, who is good at rhyming, and so on. The better you know your students, the better you can connect when they are struggling with self-control. *Miguel, remember in the game when you needed to wait until the ball was thrown? The same type of watching and responding that is needed here.*

Build relationship with student jobs

Knowing your students well—their interests, strengths, and areas for growth—helps you assign jobs that will help them develop capacity for leadership. Jobs also hand over some of the power in the classroom. Student jobs can include timekeeper, materials manager, check-in monitor, and the like.

Relationship-building conferences

Spontaneous opportunities for relationship-building occur throughout the day. *How did your soccer game end last night, Rosie? It was fun to see you at the mall yesterday, Jonny.*

You can plan conferences for the purpose of relationship-building. They allow you to grow in awareness of students' strengths and what motivates them, and you can use such knowledge to help them regulate their behavior. Your deeper knowledge and understanding of students might alter your approach to someone. Relationship-building conferences can be brief or may last a few minutes; they can happen before, during, or after classes.

During the conference, ask if the student has a preference regarding redirection: Would prefer and be able to track nonverbal cues? Is it useful for her to take a slightly longer break than is usual? If the student isn't sure, explain that redirection will be based on your observation of what has worked well or not so well in the past. Because your choice of redirection tools will be guided by this collaboration, students will be more likely to perceive your redirection as support.

Resources: For relationship-building conference steps, see *Classroom Discipline*, pages 48-51, and the *Developmental Designs 2 Resource Book*, pages 113-114.

Relationship and endorsement

Positive, trusting teacher leadership is a step toward student endorsement of behavior guidelines. Adolescents need more than trust to follow rules, even when they are created by consensus. They need to know why these guidelines are necessary: Why does this matter in my life? How is this not just a way of trying to control me? See Endorsement below for ideas.

Follow through

Once Pathways has been explained and practiced, use it! When you and your students get used to the approach, everyone will grow to appreciate it. You'll find that you spend less time and have far less stress in disciplining, and they'll see that you not only take the time to teach them the approach, you follow through: you walk the talk.

Two key points

In a conversation with a student who is struggling to respond positively to Pathways, be sure to communicate two points:

1. I'm on your side and I'll never give up on you

2. I will always enforce the rules, for you and for everyone.

The message can be communicated in as many ways as there are teachers. Vocabulary of effective, non-judgmental phrases coupled with a commitment to students' growth, no matter what flack we may get in response to our efforts, are approaches that can take many forms.

Accept the need but not the behavior

The *Developmental Designs* approach acknowledges that students will seek to fulfill their needs for fun, relationship, autonomy, and competence. We earnestly try to help them meet their needs in pro-social ways, but as they cope with dramatically changing bodies, new emotions, peer pressures, and family situations, sometimes they behave destructively. Your work to establish a relationship with a student may involve thinking deeply and observing his/her behavior closely to understand what needs s/he may be trying to meet with certain behaviors. With a foundation of observation and reflection, you can begin with confidence a conversation with the student about how to meet his/her needs in a pro-social way.

Acknowledging that students have needs is not the same as accepting all their behaviors. Be clear about this: *I know you enjoy socializing with each other, but it's individual work time now. You will have time to share your work with a partner in a few minutes.*

Resource: Review the Meeting Student Needs chart in the *Developmental Designs 1 Resource Book,* page 132, for help analyzing student behavior.

Each redirection and each problem-solving session with students who balk at the rules guides them in the right direction. Our mindsets, our trust in each other, our assumption of students' positive intentions, our faith in students' capacity for self-control, our casual chats with them to build relationship—all contribute to the conversation.

TEACHER PREPARATION

Reflect on your use of the Pathways tools

Review the Pathways tools. Which ones do you use well and whenever you need them? Are there any that you avoid using or forget? Set a goal to add one tool at a time to your repertoire. See the list descriptions of Pathways tools on page 114 of the *Developmental Designs 1 Resource Book.*

Pathways requires reflecting and analyzing. Get into the habit of thoroughly analyzing how and when you use Pathways and how students respond. *Am I intervening too soon, before students have a chance to fix it themselves? Do I wait too long before intervening?*

As reflection becomes a habit, you will gain insight, your implementation will improve, and students will appreciate the integrity of your approach. Because Pathways allows teachers to differentiate their responses to misbehavior according to students' needs, you need to observe and reflect on each student's response to various cues, especially if a student tends to respond negatively to a certain redirect. Over time and once you have a habit of reflection, you will become more and more adept at choosing redirects that students respond to successfully.

For help determining what behavior requires redirection, see Accountability/Timely and consistent response, below on page 131.

Bear in mind the four essential needs as you match redirects to students. For example, a student who wants power can be encouraged to fix mistakes quickly and effectively, without pushing back, by appealing to the fact that by doing so, he is in control of the situation—the incident can be handled now, quickly, rather than continuing the confrontation. Likewise, a student who highly values being with her peers can be encouraged to quickly fix mistakes so she can return to working with her friends. The more you think about and reflect on your Pathways practice, the better it serves you and the students.

Resources:

- Meeting Student Needs, *Development Designs 2 Resource Book*, page 132, and *Classroom Discipline*, page 280

- Read how one teacher analyzed TAB Out and Back reflection feedback and adjusted his teaching to reduce disruptions in the article *Rethinking "Take a Break Out"* by Christopher Hagedorn at www.DevelopmentalDesigns.org

What would best help him grow?

Keep your eyes on the prize throughout the year. Pathways to Self-control goal is not teachers disciplining students, but students learning the skills of self-discipline. Sometimes we forget the goal in the heat of the moment (remember your mindsets!), and bad feelings can develop on both sides. Knowing that growth happens gradually and includes slips, we acknowledge small steps toward the goal of responsible independence. This is the essence of a growth mindset. See Chapter Two:

Mindsets Create the Tone of Teaching for practical ways to nurture your growth mindset and ways to foster this mindset in students.

Investing time in year-long growth in self-management

During the first week or two of the year, you will work extra hard to introduce and implement Pathways. Teach everyone the cues you'll be using, how to respond to each one, and how to get back on track. Of course, this early focus on Pathways is not how the whole year will go! Go slow at the beginning of the year in order to go fast the rest of the year. You will need to help students maintain good habits, and return to establishing expectations as necessary, but students will grow more or less steadily in their ability to fix their mistakes. As students respond appropriately to your redirects with decreasing support from you, everybody's focus on academics increases.

Using Pathways will not take an excessive amount of your time. Once the strategies are established, they integrate smoothly into daily teaching and learning. The following two sections present ideas for increasing your skillful use of the tools so they don't disrupt the class.

Empowering language for redirection

Use respectful, neutral teacher language as you redirect. In most cases, the less you say, the more autonomy students retain and the less likely you are to get caught up in a power struggle. Explain this to students: *I want you to be in control of yourself and your day. When I redirect, I'll do so subtly and without emotion. It's up to you whether you keep it low-key.* With brevity, your message is more direct and non-negotiable: *Claire, change seats with Carl.* It takes practice to learn to use the best mindset for the situation and to speak in a neutral tone with determination, and the payoff is huge.

Here is a story about the value of brevity:

It was a warm day in early spring. A boy walking by the bank of a river could not resist the temptation to remove his clothes and plunge in for his first swim of the year, but the water was much colder and deeper than he expected. The boy was on the point of sinking when he caught sight of a man nearby.

"Help! Help!" screamed the boy. "I'm drowning! Save me!"

The traveler called out, "You foolish young man! Don't you realize it's too early to go swimming? What would your mother say if she knew you were in the river at this time of the year?! What were you thinking?!"

"Save me now, sir," interrupted the struggling boy, "and lecture me later!"

— Aesop, "The Boy Bathing"

Establishing the Pathways System

Prepare the spaces
Arrange the room so that

- you have appropriate take a break spot(s)

- there is space on the wall for the items you will need to post (goals and declarations, Social Contract, visual reminders)

- you have clear sightlines to see everybody.

TAB Out spaces: Your TAB Out partner need not be a teacher; any adult in a room nearby can receive a visiting student. Many schools create and staff a designated TAB Out room.

Plan for introducing Pathways

All students must be clear about your expectations, and they need to endorse the commitment that redirection will benefit their learning. Careful planning of the introduction of the principles and practices of Pathways is essential for its success. For ideas about modeling each redirection, see Expectations below. For strategies that help students endorse Pathways strategies, see Endorsement below.

Team approach: If possible, gather multiple classes together, e.g., all the seventh graders or everyone on a team. This is ideal when colleagues are aligned in their commitment to Pathways. It saves time and avoids repeating the introduction in each class. Present the system:

1) its goals (increased social-emotional skills, responsible independence)

2) the teacher's role

3) the student's role

4) each redirection tool teachers will use

5) how students are to respond to each tool

6) troubleshooting

7) what if's

Each teacher must clarify with her/his classes how each redirection may look and sound in his/her room (location of the TAB chair, TAB Out room, etc.).

Resources:

- To promote alignment of Pathways with your school discipline policy, see the argument for Pathways in *Classroom Discipline*, pages 135-142

- Read how tracking his use of take a break helped one teacher more effectively use this Pathways tool in the article *Take a Break: September Through May* by Jit Kundan at www.DevelopmentalDesigns.org

- Read one teacher's approach to implementing action apologies in the article *Perfecting Apologies* by Dan Calder at www.DevelopmentalDesigns.org

Special note about full problem-solving conferences: For more support in conducting these longer conferences, review the steps of a full problem-solving conference (see page 131 in *Developmental Designs 2 Resource Book*), and then plan what you will say. Write down points you want to make and questions you might ask for each step of the conference. To ensure that you have solidified your understanding of the student, use the Student Profile, page 22 in the *Developmental Designs 1 Resource Book*.

Use the Loop to reinforce Pathways introductions

After introducing and using each strategy, use the Loop to help students reflect. For example, after you've been using Fix It on the Spot for a few weeks, you might begin a class by asking: *How well are we doing with Fix It on the Spot? Thumbs up if you think we're doing well, sideways if you think we're doing OK but need some work, and thumbs down if you think it isn't going well, and we should talk about it.*

Resource: For more information about effective use of the Loop to address Pathways issues, see *Developmental Designs 1 Resource Book*, pages 5-7, and *Classroom Discipline*, pages 168 and 170.

EXPECTATIONS

Be sure all students are introduced to the Pathways system of handling rule-breaking behavior—there will have to be a make-up session for those who miss the big introduction. Every student needs to understand the system. Regardless of an individual's capacity at the moment for self-control and internal motivation, all students must be clear about what is expected of them. For many, simply establishing clear expectations will be sufficient to keep them on the right path most of the time. For some, additional work on social skills with adult mentors will be necessary. For each and every student, when they miss the mark, the rules and expectations must be enforced.

When to establish expectations

Behavior expectations for redirections need to be established, practiced, and revisited from time to time throughout the year, especially at the start of each new term and returning to school after a break. The first few weeks of the year are critical. At that time, set the behavioral expectation for one strategy—for example, take a break—immediately prior to modeling and practicing. When you are ready to teach the next strategy, set the expectations, model and practice, and so on. Use every strategy exactly the way you establish it: consistent enforcement is critical, and it's the hardest part.

Example: A teacher introduces Fix It on the Spot on Day Two of the school year, then uses it as needed for the next several weeks, adding other redirection cues at other times. If the teacher uses Fix It on the Spot consistently and exactly as it was presented, the teacher will need to use it less and less frequently as the year moves along and student behavior improves. The same is true for all of the strategies.

Modeling

Use modeling to show students exactly how you want them to respond to each redirection, including nonverbal cues, redirecting language, Loss of Privilege, take a break, Fix It on the Spot, and TAB Out and Back. To review the modeling format, see *Classroom Discipline*, pages 88-95, and the *Developmental Designs 1 Resource Book*, pages 70-73. Because endorsement is key to productive modeling, see Endorsement below for ideas on how to bring energy to the "student input" step as you model.

Think-alouds

Think-alouds teach students to process redirection and refocus. Using them when you introduce expectations models positive student response to redirection. Being able to process experiences and emotions on one's own is a fundamental skill for maintaining self-control. Give students examples of what you might be thinking if you were asked to take a break or a privilege was temporarily taken away:

Aargh! Ms. Smith doesn't miss anything in this class! She has eyes everywhere! (Sigh) Well, she did catch me. I was trying to give Sharon a note. My bad. I'll give it to her in the hall.

Now I have to work alone. This math is so hard! I hate it! I don't want to do it. But I suppose I was better off having Darien to help me instead of being stuck by myself. It's hard to work with my buddy, though. We talk too much about chess. I'll ask Mr. Shelton about a new partner tomorrow.

Resource: *Classroom Discipline*, pages 175-176, think-aloud example for TAB

Compare redirects

You can have a whole-group conversation about the redirects you will be using. This gives students a chance to think about each one, compare them, and look for similarities and differences. Students can discuss in an objective, unemotional atmosphere how misbehavior will be handled. For example:

- All require students to stop and think.

- All require students to respond quickly and quietly.

- Most require some sort of problem solving, but in many cases, simply settling down and centering oneself can go a long way toward solving a problem.

- Some require action (Fix It on the Spot, take a break, certain losses of privilege), while others do not (nonverbal cue, redirecting language, reminding language).

- Fix it on the Spot prevents a student from slipping into a negative pattern; the others may or may not.

- Every redirect works best when the teacher responds to the misbehavior quickly.

- None requires a direct apology, although some situations make one necessary. In many cases, simply regaining self-control and getting back to rule-following behavior is all that's necessary.

Power of peer influence

Seeing their peers get along and succeed is a powerful way for students to learn and reinforce the skills necessary for smooth social interaction. You can take advantage of their strong peer-orientation by having students participate in introducing Pathways. Student leadership possibilities include demonstrating think-alouds and modeling, and sharing about the benefits of building self-control. Student demonstrations of TAB combined with think-alouds can underline the value of this redirection tool and increase endorsement.

Visual reminders

A visual helps students remember a redirection routine. A Y-chart that lists what it looks like, sounds like, and feels like to take a break can be placed near the TAB chair; a list of several action apologies can serve as a menu of possibilities. A particularly helpful chart is one that clearly defines what the roles will be for student and teacher when behavior strays from the class' agreed-upon expectations. Teacher and student roles are discussed directly following, under Accountability.

Resource: See more ideas for visual reminders in the *Developmental Designs 1 Resource Book*, pages 74-75.

ACCOUNTABILITY

Accountability is a two-way street. Teachers and students work together: both are accountable for certain aspects of the system.

Teacher accountability:

- At the start of the year, teachers must thoroughly introduce Pathways: its goal, what teachers should do, what students should do, each redirection tool and how students should respond to each one, what to do if something is not working, etc.

- Teachers are expected to notice *all* student behavior and redirect rule breakers as quickly as possible, while remaining neutral and objective. Teacher response must be consistent.

- When too many students are misbehaving to allow for effective redirection of individuals, the teacher must stop the group, regain control, and review and renew commitment to the class' expectations.

- The teacher observes how students respond to various redirects, so a redirect that works well for a particular student can be used regularly for him/her. Later in the year, a tool that did not work in the past might be retried.

- When the teacher sees a student consistently respond negatively to a redirect, s/he conferences on-to-one with the individual, and together they decide on a tool that will be more effective to use. Then follow-through is critical: conferencing will be repeated as necessary.

- When negative response to redirects becomes common in the class, a problem-solving meeting is necessary, in which the class identifies the problem(s) and adopts solutions. Order, shared responsibility, and commitment to the Social Contract must be restored.

Student accountability:

- Students participate in creation of the Social Contract, then sign it, pledging to honor it.

- Students maximize their learning time and minimize their off-task time.

- Students make every effort to follow the rules throughout the class period.

- Students respond quickly, quietly, and appropriately to all teacher redirects.

- Students learn the skills of centering themselves, seeking help as necessary.

- After TAB, student reenters the regular flow of class quietly.

- Students communicate with the teacher if they choose not to or cannot respond appropriately to a redirect.

- Students think about and identify redirects that will work for them and share these perceptions with teachers.

- Students help and encourage each other when appropriate to regain self-control.

Teachers must hold students accountable for these expectations, and students must endorse them for the system to work (see Endorsement below for help fostering student investment in Pathways).

See *Developmental Designs 1 Resource Book*'s Pathways to Self-control, pages 111-135, and *Classroom Discipline*, Chapter Seven, for extensive discussion of effective use of Pathways. Once students see that you use the principles and tools of Pathways consistently and fairly, they will begin to take responsibility for regulating themselves. If student behavior starts to break down broadly, you must stop trying to teach content and spend the time it takes to repair and rebuild—*don't ignore the problem while it's small!* The longer you postpone intervention, the longer it takes to regain order and a productive climate.

Resources:

- Read strategies for diffusing power struggles in article *Student "Pushback"* by Nell Sears and Jit Kundan at www.DevelopmentalDesigns.org

- Read strategies for maintaining an effective signal for attention in the article *Reviving the Signal for Attention* at www.DevelopmentalDesigns.org

- Read strategies for constructive, equitable use of TAB in the article *Use Take a Break to Keep Students Learning* at www.DevelopmentalDesigns.org

Tune up your watchful eye

Pathways requires vigilance. The intensity of early implementation decreases after the first few weeks, but you must be ever watchful to keep students focused on learning and to maintain a positive environment.

Some ways to increase your observation skills:

- Arrange the room so you can see everything and everybody, even as you move around

- Consistently scan the room, even as you work with individuals or small groups
- Organize so you don't have to search for things while lecturing, demonstrating, or facilitating discussions—avoid setting up distractions
- Separate students who trigger each other
- Videotape or arrange to be observed, and learn whether you miss misbehavior, and if so, if there is a pattern you can change

Resource: *Classroom Discipline*, pages 33-34, "Seeing Everything, and then Acting"

Timely and consistent response maintains the authority of the Contract

If it seems unnecessary to respond to small infractions, consider the message you send when you are not consistent in responding to all student behaviors: students see that some rule breaking is tolerated. Naturally, some will test you to see how far they can get before being caught. In effect, you have recalled all the accountability to yourself, recreating the teacher-versus-students dynamic most teachers long to escape. The integrity of the Social Contract that everyone agreed to follow is badly damaged, and a great deal of rebuilding is necessary. Much better to require integrity from yourself from the beginning.

The Social Contract carries authority because it has been created through a process of consensus and because everyone in the class community individually endorsed it. Just as in life outside school, sometimes someone wishes they could take back their endorsement or be an exception to the rules, but that *must not happen.*

Every behavior that conflicts with the Contract needs to be called out and fixed. For example, if your Contract calls on endorsers to respect people, any behavior that demonstrates lack of respect must be immediately redirected by the teacher and fixed by the student.

Not all the paths in Pathways are straight and narrow, because what is ideal for one person may not be useful for another. You may not be sure exactly how you will work with a rule breaker, but it is crucially important to make it clear that you notice the behavior and it must stop, and you will address it later.

Resource: Read about the effective use of Fix It on the Spot in the article *Fix It on the Spot at Its Finest* by Christopher Hagedorn at www.DevelopmentalDesigns.org

Tracking plans from TAB Out and Back

The success of TAB Out and Back requires follow-through on the plan generated at the quick conference. Devise a system for reminding yourself and the student of the agreed-upon behavior and how the two of you will check in. The students might write a note in his/her planner. Note in your planner the day you agree to assess how the plan is working out.

ENDORSEMENT

Review *your* endorsement of Pathways

A premise of Pathways to Self-control is that every teacher response to rule-breaking uses the opportunity to teach responsibility and the skills of self-control. You *teach students self-discipline* rather than disciplining them. The success of Pathways depends on your endorsement of this basic premise. If you believe that students should be punished, even humiliated, for their mistakes, the Pathways strategies are not for you. If you use the strategies but still believe in punishment, students will understand that they are being punished, and that it's still teacher-versus-students. In the short run, the teacher may "win" the battle, but in the long run, the student has learned far less.

Resources: For more about the premise of Pathways, see pages 135-142 in *Classroom Discipline* and pages 107-109 in *Developmental Designs 1 Resource Book.*

It's worth the work

Teach students how to perform routines in ways that help fulfill the Contract and allow everyone in the room to learn better and to get along. Shouldn't students already know how to enter a classroom, listen respectfully, quiet down, use materials respectfully, hand in their work, and so on? Perhaps. But unless we connect our clear expectations to the Social Contract we all created and endorsed, some will not get it right. If we teach the steps, providing the learning they need to shift to productive learning habits, there is a much greater likelihood of students operating according to the Contract and succeeding socially and academically.

Foster Student Endorsement of Pathways

If what we do and why we do it seems babyish or unnecessary to students, they will resist. Explain your reasoning when appropriate (not in response to their demands or bad behavior), and involve students in decision-making and problem-solving in both the rule-making and rule-enforcing processes. This shows them respect and speaks to their needs for autonomy and competence, and they are more likely to make good choices.

Social Contract and routines

The following set of questions can help create endorsement for the Social Contract and classroom routines. Each question invites students to look inward for reasons to endorse the behavioral goals.

What is the purpose of attending school?

What are your personal goals?

Why is it important to _____?

What will be the payoffs?

To help us achieve our goals, what should _____ look, sound, and feel like?

In addition to reflection questions, you can use storytelling, personal examples, metaphors, quotes, and movie clips to help students understand and connect to the benefits of positive behavior.

Resource: For stories that help students reflect on behavior, see *Classroom Discipline,* pages 282-283

Self-management

Help students make the connection between the autonomy they want and their behavior. Ask them whether they would rather manage their own behavior or have someone else manage it for them (!). Explain your role in helping them self-manage:

They manage their own behavior by asking them to *It's important to be able to manage your own behavior, and much better to do so than have someone else manage it for you. I'm the adult who sits in the passenger seat while you learn to drive a car. I'll use the emergency brake when I see that you are going off the road, but you are in the driver's seat as long as you respond well and quickly.*

Say that you will sweat the small stuff, and explain why

Clarify your intention: *I intervene early, for little things. This may feel strict, harsh, or like I'm picking on you. But when we deal with small problems right away, we don't have to fix larger problems later.*

Help students see that tending to small infractions is part of your commitment to their learning, the goal of the Contract. Offer a real-life metaphor:

I am committed to your growth, just as I am committed to the growth of my garden over the summer. I add nutrients to the soil, I water, and I pull out weeds that would eventually choke the plants. Baby weeds seem so little they couldn't do much harm, but I know from experience that in a week or two a weed can take over the garden. Likewise, behavior that violates our Contract, left unchecked, can distract the whole class if I don't pay attention.

Explain that your redirections for small mistakes are not punitive, but supportive. When students quickly get themselves back on track after being redirected, their autonomy is restored.

Fair is not necessarily the same or equal

Because people are not alike, what works well for one student may not work for another. Students notice different responses for similar misbehavior, and this may seem unfair to them. Share some examples that show why fair is not always the same:

- Two students, Kathy and Al, side-talk during a lesson. Kathy is sitting next to someone she frequently side-talks to, so you have her move to a different place. Al has a habit of side-talking to anyone near him, so you have him take a break so he can think about it and work on breaking his habit when he returns.

- Two students using classroom computers slam them shut. Aleisha did so out of frustration because she couldn't find what she needed, and Thomas did so because he was clowning around. You decide that Aleisha will lose the privilege of using the computers until you and she have a conference to help her plan to control her emotions better, and Thomas must take a break to stop clowning and refocus.

Explain that you will adjust your responses throughout the year, always using one that fits the moment and the person: *When someone consistently does not respond well to a redirect, I'll talk to him or her about it, so we can figure out something that will work.*

Stories and Language to Seek Endorsement

Take a break
Everyone needs to get away from the action sometimes so they can calm down and relax. During the making of a movie or a TV show, every once in a while, the director says, 'Take five!' Everyone takes a short break to rest, adjust their wigs, whatever. In our classroom, this will be our 'Take five' spot.

In hockey, when a referee sees a player break a rule, he calls him on it, and the player has to sit out for a couple of minutes. The rule-breaker doesn't get thrown out of the game or fined or suspended: just a couple of minutes off the ice. Then he rejoins the game. That's how take a break works, but this is not a penalty box—it's a centering chair.

Resource: Read how to help students experience TAB constructively in the article *Yep, Everyone Needs a Break* by Eric Charlesworth at www.DevelopmentalDesigns.org

Nonverbal cues
Explain that nonverbal cues are the best kind, because they're quick, quiet, and discreet. *Think of orchestra conductors. Nearly all of their directions are nonverbal. They hardly speak at all during a performance, but they give a lot of nonverbal direction, and the result is beautiful music. I hope we can communicate effectively nonverbally, too.*

Fix it on the Spot
When you make a mistake, sometimes the best thing I can do is give you a chance to get it right on your own, quickly and quietly, so your mistake doesn't become a habit. For example, if you start to address the class and your voice isn't loud enough, I might stop you right away and ask you to begin again, with more volume to your voice, or someone might signal you by putting a hand to their ear. That's fixing it on the spot.

Redirecting language
Sometimes you need to know exactly what I want you to do to fix something. In that case, I'll tell you straight and clear, so there is no doubt. I might say, 'Frank, put down the scissors and pay attention.'

Reminding language
Sometimes it's best if you figure it out yourself, rather than have me tell you the solution. I might ask you a leading question or in some other way guide your thinking so you can solve it yourself—for instance, 'José, what should you be doing right now?'

Loss of Privilege

When you've been given a privilege and aren't handling it well, I might temporarily take away that privilege so you can pull yourself together and plan how you'll keep the privilege when it's returned. Once the privilege is restored, you'll have a better understanding of how to use the privilege appropriately. One of the worst things I can do is nothing at all, allowing you to continue to abuse the privilege. That's bad for everyone. If one person can abuse a privilege, then anyone in the room can, and soon we'd have chaos.

Quick conference

Sometimes it's possible to confer with a student right away, so we can discuss a mistake he or she has made. I can't always do this—often, I'm busy with others—but when it's possible, a quick conference can clear up a misunderstanding or make a quick plan for better teamwork next time.

ENGAGEMENT

Build the habit of reflecting on behavior

You can use the Loop to discover what behavior promotes learning or promotes achievement of goals:

This year, I've added the Loop to my teaching habits. After the lesson, and just before we head for the lab, I ask a student to remind us of our safety rules, or how we're going to proceed in the lab. When we conclude an experiment, instead of just checking to make sure they have their homework assignment written in their planners, I have them circle up, and we review what we learned. I ask, 'What did we learn today?' 'What's important about what we learned?' 'Who remembers what we're going to do tomorrow?' We close lab time by looking ahead, planning for next time.

—High school teacher, Red Lake MN (from *Classroom Discipline*)

You can focus on specific aspects of behavior such as regaining self-control. For a class period or during a particular activity, ask students to note moments of distraction when they needed to refocus on learning. Then use the Loop to share why their control slipped and successful strategies for getting back on track. Math classes could collect statistics or create bar graphs to chart the patterns; social studies classes could analyze causes and effects in social behaviors.

Use the Loop in one-to-one exchanges: *You're about to regain the privilege of using our computers, Aleisha. I know you can handle it. Before you start, tell me how you'll use the computer from now on.*

As she begins to exercise the restored privilege, reinforce positive things you notice about how she's doing, and help her plan how she'll avoid repeating her mistake: *You're visiting the correct site, and I can see you're staying out of iTunes. Keep it up, even if you get a little bored. What will you do if you're tempted to move off your task and use the computer in ways that are not within our guidelines?*

At the end of her session, reflect with her on what she did to stay within the guidelines: *Finished, Aleisha? How was it? What did you do to keep yourself focused?*

Use the Loop to boost conferences: Many Pathways tools have reflection built into their steps to realize the highest engagement and understanding possible in the student. Conferences about behavior are greatly enriched by asking students to reflect. Conferences are times to show your support—your desire to learn about and provide what the student needs, increasing the chance that the student will open his or her mind and think hard as you problem-solve.

Consider this exchange from *Classroom Discipline*, page 195, for Step Two of full problem-solving conferences:

Brainstorm solutions: Ask the student what is needed to avoid rule breaking and offer suggestions if needed.

What do you need to do to keep yourself focused and working in here, Darian? You said you wanted to pass every subject this year. What can you do to make that happen?

Would it help if I gave you a starter question as soon as you come into class? Do you need to talk to an adult about anything going on in your life? I could arrange that for you.

If a student needs help generating ideas, keep a list of what has helped others and draw from it. You could recall supports that helped you as an adolescent, or currently. It may be encouraging to the student that others have struggled and then succeeded.

Acknowledge strengths

Acknowledge success in abiding by the rules in the moment and at the end of the class period. Positive reinforcement encourages appropriate school behavior and students' moral development. "Teachers who help their students feel good about learning through classroom successes, friendships, and celebrations are doing the very things the student brain craves."[1]

Talk about the behaviors you see that support the rules. Connect specific helpful actions to the rules they support. Students need to see the connections. Make connections verbally when you notice them. They provide students with immediate feedback for steady growth.

In-the-moment affirmations: When things are going well, mention it (this is especially important in the first two months of school), and name the relevant rule or modeled procedure: *I notice all the small groups are on task and holding lively discussions. You're being respectful and responsible, and you're doing your best! We'll get a lot of learning done this year.*

I notice everyone is listening the way we modeled it. That's going to help us learn a lot.

Almost everyone had an answer ready when I called on him or her during discussion time.

You might also acknowledge successes at the beginning and end of class periods. If you have created charts to remind everyone what abiding by the rules looks, sounds, and feels like, you and students may add to the ever growing list of the behaviors to support the rules you notice.

Whole group acknowledgment: Involve students in quick celebrations of their strengths. For example, if students have been collaborating well, note how their co-operation supports the efficiency and productivity of the class, and add a cheer such as Clap on Three: at the count of three, everyone claps once, exactly in unison. The difficulty of getting it exactly right highlights the challenge of cooperating!

Resource: See Acknowledgments and Cheers in Educator Help at www. DevelopmentalDesigns.org and on pages 213-215 of *The Advisory Book*

Use stories and metaphors

The Endorsement section above includes examples of language that inspires interest in developing positive learning behavior with Pathways tools. You can add to these resources a story about when you shifted from external control by adults to internal control to meet the demands of school, or in a sport or hobby, or another personal goal.

Sample story for reflection

Stories like the one below appear in Chapters Seven and Eight of *Classroom Discipline*. Their meanings are open-ended, designed to prompt students to reflect on their behavior.

The Farmer and the Donkey

A donkey wandered away from its owner when the farmer wasn't looking, went down a slippery slope, and fell into a ravine. The farmer tried to help him get out, but the donkey was too heavy. Then he had an idea. The farmer got a shovel, and, talking encouragingly to the donkey, began to shovel dirt into the ravine. Some of the dirt fell on the donkey, who didn't like it very much, and for a moment the donkey even thought the farmer was attempting to punish him by burying him alive! But slowly, as the farmer kept shoveling and kept encouraging the donkey to shake it off and step up on the dirt, the donkey realized that the dirt was rising higher and higher. "Come on, I know you can do it!" said the farmer. "Shake it off and step up!" The donkey shook the dirt off its back and stepped up on the dirt the farmer shoveled in, and saw that he had made considerable progress in extricating himself from his difficult position. "Come on, keep going, you're almost here!" said the farmer. "Shake it off and step up, and soon you'll be out of the hole!"

The donkey took his advice, shook the dirt off his back, and stepped up onto the dirt the farmer shoveled in. Finally, he was able to walk out of the ravine to freedom.

Story discussion: After reading the story, discuss similarities between the story and classroom redirections:

- The donkey made a mistake; students (and everyone else) make mistakes and break rules
- The farmer helped the donkey fix its mistake; teachers help students fix their mistakes

- The donkey was uncomfortable with the farmer's help felt at first; getting a redirection from a teacher feels uncomfortable
- The farmer encouraged the donkey to be resilient and keep working at it; correcting behavior teaches students resilience and perseverance
- The donkey shook off the dirt and steps up; students shake off setbacks and step up to the next task; in both cases, caring adults are there to help.

Students who shut down when adults give guidance (by putting their heads down or sulking or avoiding work, etc.), rather than bouncing back, need to grow more resilient. Teachers can use the Farmer and Donkey story to offer the "shake it off and step up" model for accepting help.

Adjust redirections to fit individuals

The classroom community changes constantly: students change developmentally; their home situations change; curriculum demands change; group dynamics change over time and in response to events. Students' needs for supports to stay on track can change, too. For example, if a student stops using TAB productively, have a quick conference with him or her to learn whether the student knows why, and then consider whether a new redirect is needed.

---

1 Eric Jensen, *Teaching with the Brain in Mind* (Alexandria, VA: ASCD, 2005), 77.

ABOUT THE AUTHORS

Todd Bartholomay is the Programs and Special Projects Director for The Origins Program. He taught at the middle level for fourteen years in the Mahtomedi and St. Paul, Minnesota, public schools, and he coordinated gifted and talented services in the St. Paul district. He served for four years as assistant principal at a comprehensive high school in St. Paul, and he was principal of a K-12 school for five years there, guiding educators in instructional best practices and school reform. He has facilitated *Developmental Designs* workshops for eight years. He has a B.A. from St. Olaf College, Northfield, Minnesota and a Masters of Education, Curriculum and Instruction, from St. Thomas University, St. Paul, Minnesota.

Dr. Scott Tyink is a *Developmental Designs* consultant for The Origins Program. He taught fifth through eighth grades for 14 years. He co-organized, directed, and taught in one of Wisconsin's first multiage middle-level charter schools, where he developed a curriculum of integrated arts and technology. He has facilitated *Developmental Designs* workshops and consulted in middle schools for ten years. His current work includes writing a book on effective group work in school and piloting a program to coach teachers through on-line video. He has B.S. from the University of Wisconsin-Stout and a Masters of Education, Professional Development, from the University of Wisconsin, La Crosse, and an Ed. D. from Fielding Graduate University, Santa Barbara, California.

Erin Klug is the Program Development Specialist and a *Developmental Designs* consultant for The Origins Program. She taught in Minneapolis schools for ten years, where she practiced the *Developmental Designs* approach with success. She has taught grades three through eight and middle level math and science. She helps develop and facilitates *Developmental Designs* workshops, and as a consulting teacher, she guides implementation of the approach in middle-level schools. She has a B.A. from the University of Michigan and a Masters of Education from the University of Minnesota.

Additional *Developmental Designs* Resources

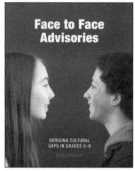

Face to Face Advisories: Bridging Cultural Gaps in Grades 5-9

Linda Crawford

Lead advisory conversations about culture to build appreciation for diversity and reduce bias.

368 pages soft cover book, 978-0-938541-20-2

New e-book! Leader's Guide to Face to Face Advisories
36 pages, 978-0-938541-22-6

Classroom Discipline: Guiding Adolescents to Responsible Independence

Linda Crawford and Christopher Hagedorn

Build a classroom climate where students practice positive behavior, help develop daily routines, and endorse expectations. Proactively guide behavior with engaging instruction. Teach self-management and minimize escalation when you redirect rule breaking.

304-page soft cover book, 978-0-938541-13-4

The Advisory Book: Building a Community of Learners Grades 5-9, Revised

Linda Crawford

Discover how advisory meets adolescents' developmental needs through two meeting formats and 200+ activities, greetings, and shares. Includes a year's worth of ready-to-use advisories on themes, such as getting acquainted, social skills, and bullying.

304-page soft cover book, 978-0-938541-21-9

Classroom Discipline Study Guide

A professional development guide and read-along for *Classroom Discipline*. Enrich your staff and team meetings and create consistent, positive behavior across classrooms. Includes meeting outlines and leader instructions.

84-page soft cover book, 978-0-938541-18-9

The Advisory Book Study Guide

This companion to *The Advisory Book* steers you chapter by chapter as you read it as a team or staff. Together, you will deepen your understanding of the advisory formats and learn how to embed them in your school.

72-page soft cover book, 978-0-938541-14-1

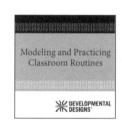

Modeling and Practicing Classroom Routines DVD

Watch educators model expectations and get students on board to create an orderly learning environment. See success in common classroom routines, including: transitions, small group work, and waiting for assistance.

38-minute DVD and viewing guide, 978-0-938541-19-6

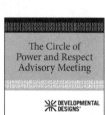

The Circle of Power and Respect Advisory Meeting DVD

See CPR in action! Watch students thoroughly engaged in advisory greetings, sharing, and games. Hear educators discuss their process and success with CPR.

70-minute DVD and viewing guide, 978-0-938541-16-5

Tried and True Classroom Games and Greetings

A dozen acknowledgments and cheers, 50 games and greetings, and more! Energize, engage, and connect adolescents through the power of play.

72-page ring bound, 978-0-938541-15-8

Order at www.developmentaldesigns.org or call (800) 543-8715   M-F: 9-5, CT

WORKSHOPS • CONSULTING • BOOKS & RESOURCES